GW00863157

Smile

'*Smile!* reinforces the importance of SPID's work in tirelessly championing the communities of North Kensington. Thompson's moving play reveals the true human impact of the contradictions and failings of local and national Government. It is a potent reminder of the questions society must urgently ask – before change is too late'

Madani Younis, Artistic Director,
formerly at Bush Theatre

Helena Thompson
Writer

Helena Thompson is an award-winning script writer and Artistic Director of S.P.I.D. Theatre. She studied playwriting under David Edgar at Birmingham University and English at Cambridge University, and was on the National Theatre's attachment scheme. Her plays for BBC Radio 4 include *The Burning Times* (*Ivy*) (*Radio Times' Pick of the Week*) and *Superyou*. Her sell-out play *Arthur's World* (Bush Theatre) is published by Oberon. Her interactive experience *iAm* (nominated for an Offie award) toured the Arcola, Southwark Playhouse and Bush Theatre. Her play *The Burning Tower* (Bush Theatre) toured estates UK wide. Her other plays include *Bluebeard's Wives* (ICA) and *Open House* (Riverside Studios, Time Out Critic's Choice). Her short film *High Above the Sky* (ITV First Light Best Film Award) has won two distribution deals, three prizes and over a hundred festival screenings worldwide.

Mel Cook
Director

Mel Cook is an experiential theatre maker. She has created festival work for Latitude, Glastonbury, LIFT, and Hide & Seek, and developed site-sympathetic work for Shunt Vaults, BAC, V&A, and The Lowry. She is Associate Director for S.P.I.D. and Coney. Mel has been a finalist for the JMK, ITV, Channel 4, Arches, Bankside, and Leverhulme directing awards. Credits include Southwark Playhouse, Arcola and Finborough.

S.P.I.D. Theatre Company

Helena Thompson founded the award-winning company S.P.I.D. (Social Progressive Interconnected Diverse) in 2005 to champion high quality community theatre on council estates. The charity works on estates throughout London and the UK creating youth shows, professional shows, youth films and tours. Shows bring audiences together using immersive, participatory, promenade or site-specific techniques. Prizes include *Time Out* Critic's Choice, an Offie Award nomination, Fringe Report's Best Outreach Company and ITV First Light Best Film Award. Coverage includes BBC, ITV, London Live and National press. S.P.I.D. is based in the historic Kensal House estate ten minutes from Grenfell Tower. The charity advocates against the destruction of social housing and fights for increased investment in estates and to improve rights for those who live and work there. S.P.I.D. are proud to announce that they have raised £2.6 million to refurbish their own neglected, historic council estate community rooms.

Remembering Grenfell

The Story of Fires and Floods toured UK estates, theatres, schools and universities June/July 2022 to commemorate the fifth anniversary of the Grenfell Tower fire. It was produced by SPID Theatre (Social Progressive Interconnected Diverse) which is based in Kensal House estate close to Grenfell. The interactive talk – the third of SPID's plays about Grenfell – was performed by SPID's Artistic Director Helena Thompson, with voices recorded by local residents. It happened alongside nationwide youth productions of the first two plays in the trilogy, *The Burning Tower* and *Smile!* You can experience it here: https://tinyurl.com/storyoffiresandfloods

Smile!

by Helena Thompson

methuen & co

First published in Great Britain in paperback by Methuen & Co 2021
This revised edition published 2022

1

Methuen & Co Ltd
Orchard House
Railway Street
Slingsby, York, YO62 4AN
www.methuen.co.uk

Methuen & Co Ltd Reg. No. 05278590

A CIP catalogue record for this title is
available from the British Library

ISBN: 978 0 413 77857 4

Typeset in Great Britain by SX Composing DTP, Rayleigh, Essex
Printed and bound in Great Britain by Clays Ltd, Elcograf S.p.A.

Smile!

Performances

Smile! is a new play commissioned by the University of Chichester to address social justice. It is the sequel to *The Burning Tower*, which dramatised the Grenfell fire's legacy and continues to be studied and performed UK wide. *Smile!* premiered at Kensal House Council Estate from 24th to 28th August 2021 and was produced by S.P.I.D. Theatre's Kai Garma with Max Graef as Head of Sound.

Cast

The Examiner	Phil Philmar
Master of Discipline	Pete Picton
Vice	Daniel Godfrey
Assistant	Leda Hodgson
Instructor	Nick Frentz
Quatro 7 Rosie	Catherine Roberts
Quatro 6 Dawn	Lia Harlin
Quatro 9 Paula	Melanie Wilder
Quatro 8 Beth	Chloe Watkinson
Quatro 22 Cat	Esme Mahoney
Mono 16 Alex	Nikoletta Soumelidis
Mono 15 Matty	Francesca Sauer
Mono 14 Anita	Lucy Bond
Mono 8 Rachel	Lakeisha Lynch-Stevens
Mono 2 Ray	Fiona McKinnon

Duration

A single act play of seventy minutes duration for stage or radio.

Set

A secure unit in an offshore correction facility on the Island of Coraim Berdu. The unit is monitored by a surveillance camera, which is connected to an automated tannoy. On a desk is an old boom box, a large display screen and stack of high-tech smiling masks. Four mattresses with bedding are on the floor, one in each corner. A leak drips into a bucket. Seating in the round.

Characters

Staff [all wearing gold, all apparently male]:

The Examiner	masks his sadism with irreverent flamboyance
Master of Discipline	inclined to simplify, idealistic
Vice Examiner ('Vice')	smug, with a great respect for rules
Assistant	ambitious yet prone to self-loathing, turns out to be a woman
Instructor	scatty yet brave, also very kind, turns out to be an Islander

Quatro trainees [all wearing black]:

Quatro 7 Rosie	born on the Island, working class, sarcastic, inclined to lead
Quatro 6 Dawn	married an Islander, has a strong maternal instinct
Quatro 9 Paula	born on the Island, self-assured, gifted with powers of intuition
Quatro 8 Beth	born on the Island, anxious, passionate despite seeming shy
Quatro 22 Cat	born on the Island, well spoken, riotous

Mono trainees [all wearing white]:

Mono 16 Alex	well spoken, witty, turns out to have more backbone than her sycophancy suggests
Mono 15 Matty	well spoken, easily over-whelmed, turns out to be a caring mother
Mono 14 Anita	well spoken, judgemental yet insightful and concerned for others

| **Mono 8 Rachel** | born on the Island, well spoken, open minded |
| **Mono 2 Ray** | working class, ballsy yet vulnerable |

Directions

* denotes the most crucial stage directions and special effects

/ indicates where the next character interrupts to speak over another character

The rhythm of the language is designed to drive the pace of the action forward.
The Security 'offstage' on page 65 should be pre-recorded.
The 'voice' of the automated tannoy is a sound effect.

Time

The play builds in real time from apparent naturalism to something more heightened.

Thanks

Smile! is dedicated to Nnenna, Byron, Olivia, Julia, Kai and Sean.

Act One

[*As the audience arrive (and/or over credits) **Quatro 6 Dawn** and **Quatro 9 Paula** can be seen, wearing regulation black. The sound of the sea can be heard, then a door slams as someone enters the facility]

Quatro 9 Paula [admiring] . . . Sister, it's like a tiny earth . . . ah the colours . . .

Quatro 6 Dawn He always liked green and blue . . . Is five too old for marbles?

Quatro 9 Paula 'course not . . . [Lowered voice, remembering] . . . picked us some yangle, thought we'd smoke it tomorrow? [Worried] . . . Dawn?

Quatro 6 Dawn [warning her off] . . . I'm OK . . . I'm OK. [**Paula** sets about adjusting the mattresses so hers is closer to **Dawn**] [Sad] . . . He won't remember me, Pauls.

Quatro 9 Paula 'course he will. You're his mum.

Quatro 6 Dawn My poor husband. They know we're Yothis and they punish us for it! The karrs are drowning before they flower, there's gargrils need bringing in, and he's stuck reading bedtime stories? He must hate me.

Quatro 9 Paula He loves you. Your boy loves you.

Quatro 6 Dawn I've missed everything, Pauls

Quatro 9 Paula Not his first word . . . chomping down on his coshu?

Quatro 6 Dawn [cheered] '. . . Wubbub.'

Quatro 9 Paula 'Wubbub.'

Quatro 6 Dawn Love you, sister

Quatro 9 Paula Love you too . . .

Quatro 6 Dawn Pauls I know I wasn't born here . . . but that woman . . . she haunts me . . . I know you see her . . . what do you see?

Quatro 9 Paula Her colours are beautiful . . . like a rainbow . . .

Quatro 6 Dawn I was thinking . . . my husband taught me the song . . . should we sing it for her?

[**Quatros 9 Paula** *and* **6 Dawn** *kneel, stretching their arms out to each other but not touching. They sing the island mourning song*]

Quatro 9 Paula & Quatro 6 Dawn [*to the tune of* Sing a Rainbow]

Wubbub Berdu sitar cree
Puidhe blinny a blee
Halarth clan ye –

[**Keys jangle*]

[**Gates unlock*

Enter **Quatro 7 Rosie** *and* **Instructor**

Rosie *wears regulation black and a mask. The* **Instructor**, *in gold uniform minus the regulation jacket, is disheveled and carries a touch-screen tablet.*

Quatro 7 Rosie [*out of breath, working class*] . . . Ten fucking flights for a piss . . .

[**Gates close*

Quatro 7 Rosie . . . Gonna unlock this fucker or what?

Instructor [*out of breath*] . . . Just a moment.

Quatro 7 Rosie I don't see any other sisters masked up?

Quatro 9 Paula [**as* **Instructor** *unclicks* **Rosie***'s mask*] . . . Give a brother a chance . . . he covered the camera, didn't he?

Quatro 6 Dawn Sir, will you get in trouble?

Instructor Just don't let me forget my jacket . . . that would be quite an error, today of all days . . . as you were, ladies. Do continue.

Quatro 9 Paula We were singing the mourning.

Instructor I'm so sorry you couldn't attend this afternoon. The ceremony on the beach was . . . I'd love to hear you. You too, Rosie. Unless you'd rather . . . ?

Quatro 7 Rosie I'll sing.

Quatro 9 Paula In English then, sisters.

[*All clear throats, kneel with hands outstretched but not touching*]

Quatros 9 Paula / 7 Rosie / 6 Dawn [*to the tune of* Sing a Rainbow]

Beloved Berdu sister true
Purple and orange and blue
Breathing words we sing you free
Island heartbeat help us see

[*middle eight*]
You are here in sea and fire
You are near in earth and air
In the flowers growing higher
In forgiveness, grace and care

[*to the tune of the first verse*]
Future colours bleed from you
Golden pasts and ripples blue
Land below and sky above
What survives . . . is love

Quatro 9 Paula . . . You alright, sir?

Instructor [*moved*] . . . I was just, er . . . thinking about Quatro 8.

Quatro 6 Dawn Hope her reading thing's going ok.

Quatro 7 Rosie What the fuck business of theirs is it if Beth can read or not?

Instructor I did try to get her exempted, but they class 'reading out loud' under language and behaviour. We all know how low she's been lately. Please help me make sure she doesn't bail on the exam.

Quatro 6 Dawn Wait . . . but you said it was just a tick-box?

Instructor It's still important to take part.

Quatro 7 Rosie [*flumping on the mattress*] . . . Time for a kip . . . [**As water splashes her face*] . . . Uhh! . . . What the . . . [*Leaping up*] . . . under the fucking leak?

Instructor Quatro 6, Quatro 9, I think Quatro 7 deserves to know why you moved her mattress.

Quatro 9 Paula Sorry . . . we wanted to be closer. My / powers

Quatro 7 Rosie Fuck your 'powers', sis!

Instructor Please put the mattresses back in their corners – the Examiner favours a performative approach, apparently; we might need some form of seating . . . [**Paula** *and* **Dawn** *drag mattresses and move the bucket*] . . . While you're doing that, quick practice . . . Quatro 6, what should Quatro 7 have said?

Quatro 6 Dawn "Thanks for dragging my mattress under the fucking leak"?

Instructor Almost . . . drop the negative?

Quatro 9 Paula "Thanks for dragging my mattress under the leak"?

Instructor Perfect.

Quatro 7 Rosie If you're a sarky bitch . . .

Instructor Okay then. Now I almost forgot, ladies. The Examiner requested music for today . . . [*Moving to hit play*] . . . I thought of you when I made this playlist . . . I hope you like it . . . hang on . . .

[*Music can be heard*: Lovely Day *by Bill Withers*]

Instructor . . . I have some small leaving gifts for you ladies . . . [*Passing round fruit*] . . . fresh from the Island.

Quatro 9 Paula Kandrils! You used to live on these, right Rosie?

Quatro 7 Rosie . . . When I was three . . .

Quatro 6 Dawn [*taking fruit*] . . . My boy loved them. Guzzled half we grew. Thanks, sir. [*Girls eat and pass on*]

Quatro 7 Rosie [*spitting*] . . . Yeah, 'Thanks'

Instructor [*concerned*] . . . Oh, are they . . . another chance to practice?

Quatro 9 Paula [*spitting*] 'Interesting.'

Quatro 7 Rosie If by interesting you mean fucking sour.

Instructor I'll chuck them . . .

Quatro 6 Dawn I don't get it . . . Berdu fruit was always the sweetest . . .

Quatro 7 Rosie Was is the word . . .

Quatro 9 Paula Sisters, the land has been broken, earth from water. It's not the Yothi way.

Quatro 6 Dawn Everything's separate now, my husband says. Draining, planting, something to do with their budgets. It doesn't work. And if we can't grow, how will we eat?

Instructor I believe it's mainly . . . [*Beep] . . . imports now . . .

Quatro 9 Paula Sir, your screen just beeped

Instructor [*checking screen*] . . . Did it? [**Turning music off*] . . . Don't forget your Smiles?

Quatro 7 Rosie Not again

Instructor [*distributing 'Smile' masks*] . . . Remember, the wiring is delicate

Quatro 7 Rosie [**click as* **Instructor** *locks on the mask*] 'til it fucking shocks your face off

Quatro 6 Dawn [**click . . . click*] . . . These holes are too small.

Quatro 9 Paula Sir, your jacket?

Instructor Oh. Right . . . final reminder then . . . the one word the Examiner will not allow / is

Quatro 6 Dawn Don't say it!

Quatro 9 Paula It's bad luck, brother?

Instructor But we're all clear?

Quatro 7 Rosie Clear as fuck. 'Big fucking grins'?

Instructor Right . . . I'm uncovering the camera.

[*****Master of Discipline** *punches entry code in from outside*]

[*As the *gates open, the* **Instructor** *hurriedly puts on his jacket*]

Enter **Master of Discipline**, *marching in – panting – wearing a gold uniform, glasses and carrying a touch-screen tablet and gun*

Enter **Quatro 22 Cat**, *wearing a mask and in regulation black – also panting.*

Master of Discipline [*breathlessly*] . . . Instructor . . . shambolic . . . attire!

Instructor [*hurriedly adjusting his jacket*] . . . Apologies

[**Gates close*

Master of Discipline I am the Master! The Master of Discipline! I know the code! I never forget! Numbers are colours! Six for blue! I will not tell you the code!

Instructor Right. Yes, best keep that to yourself.

Quatro 7 Rosie [*lowered voice*] '. . . You fucking moron.'

Master of Discipline I am the man with the gun! My gun has three bullets! I protect the Examiner! Where is the Examiner?

Instructor He's, er . . . not arrived yet.

Master of Discipline Oh. Quatro . . . [**Beep*] . . . read your error!

Quatro 22 Cat [*reading from display screen, well spoken*] '. . . Quatro 22 . . . impeding income generation.'

Quatro 6 Dawn [*lowered voice*] . . . Is she really a four?

Quatro 7 Rosie . . . Black don't suit you, 'darling'!

Quatro 9 Paula [*lowered voice*] . . . Hang on . . . She's that girl . . . her dad sold Berdu?

Instructor [**beep*] . . . Trainees, I've just been beeped an update . . . [*Reading*] . . . Due to faulty electrics on floor 36 and the current unavailability of contractors, Quatro 22 will be sharing this unit.

Master of Discipline Trainees, Mantra!

Quatros 6 Dawn, 7 Rosie, 9 Paula, 22 Cat [*enthusiastically*] Smile! Support! Say yes!

Assistant [*rattling the gate*] . . . Hello? . . . Hi?

Master of Discipline I am the Master! I know the code! Who are you?

Assistant I'm the Assistant. There's been a flood on floor 4. I've brought Monos 14, 15 and 16 to spend their last night with you. Could you let us in please?

[****Master of Discipline** *punches in entry code*]

Gates open

Enter **Assistant**, *wearing a uniform and carrying a
touch-screen tablet*

Enter (with the **Assistant**) **Mono 14 Anita**, **Mono 15 Matty**
and **Mono 16 Alex**,
all wearing regulation white and masks

Quatro 7 Rosie [*lowered voice*] . . . And the 'angels' wear
white . . .

[*Gates close*

Quatro 7 Rosie . . . Flying in to 'save' us? [*As* **Paula** *kicks
her*] . . . Ow!

Master of Discipline Monos . . . [*Beep*] . . . read your
errors!

Mono 14 Anita [*well spoken, reading from display screen*]
' . . . Mono14: opposing improvements.'

Mono 15 Matty [*well spoken, reading from display screen*]
' . . . Mono 15: inciting negativity.'

Mono 16 Alex [*well spoken, reading from display screen*]
' . . . Mono 16: spreading sadness.'

Assistant As the Assistant, may I congratulate you on
completing your training. My understanding is that you
Quatros have had the privilege of four years' instruction,
whilst Monos' correction has lasted just one year.

Quatro 7 Rosie 'My heart bleeds'

[*From outside,* **Vice Examiner** *begins to punch in the entry code*]

[*Master* *rushes to enter the code himself*]

[*Rattling can be heard as digits are punched in*]

Vice Examiner We've been through this! It won't open if we both try to code-in at once, Master!

Master of Discipline I am the Master! You are the Vice!

*Gate opens

Master of Discipline . . . I know the code!

Enter **Vice Examiner**, *huffing and puffing,*
wearing a gold uniform and carrying a touch-screen tablet

Vice Examiner [*out of breath*] '. . . Thank you, Master!' . . . Greelu, trainees! . . . [*Silence*] . . . Quatros, am I mispronouncing . . . 'greelu'?

[**Gate closes*

Quatro 22 Cat Greila is Island greetings, brother.

Vice Examiner The Master and I have recently returned from the Examiner's worldwide tour promoting this facility. During that time I was lucky enough to benefit from a course in Berdu.

Instructor Excuse me, where is the Examiner?

Vice Examiner His last exam ran over slightly. I'm next in command.

Master of Discipline I'm next in command!

Vice Examiner Gosh yes, we both are extremely important. We both know the code. The access-all-areas code. Instructors only get unit keys, and Assistants can't open gates at all! . . . [*To* **Trainees**] . . . The Master is here to discipline – rules and incentives are my area. The extremely successful 'Report-a-Frown' initiative, for example? That was my idea.

Instructor How long is the Examiner likely to be, Vice?

Vice Examiner That's really not your concern. He's briefed me to check you're all up to speed regarding the exam.

Instructor The impression he gave me is that the exam is a bonding activity designed to affirm positivity and empathy on the trainees' last day.

Vice Examiner Oh dear. An exam is not about bonding, instructor. I hope you're taking this seriously.

Assistant Correct me if I'm wrong, but this corporation's ability to maximise happiness strikes me as absolutely vital at this tough time.

Vice Examiner Watch this one, Instructor . . . he'll have your job.

Instructor Excuse me, but what exactly will the exam involve?

Master of Discipline Exams are top secret!

Assistant I'd imagine the aim will be to prove an understanding of Smile's positivity, its resilience as a diverse ecosystem. This facility, the extraction program, and our support of Coraim Berdu's magnificent government, all positively sustain each other. Trainee language is corrected, peace is maintained, and the Island stays solvent.

Quatro 9 Paula [*lowered voice*] . . . if by peace you mean mass civilian shootings

Quatro 7 Rosie [*lowered voice*] . . . if by solvent you mean corrupt as fuck

Quatro 22 Cat [*lowered voice*] . . . if by Island you mean idiots like my father

Vice Examiner To recap then: race, class . . . what about gender?

Master of Discipline Strong, positive females of the future!

Vice Examiner 'Thank you, Master.' Yes extensive trialling found that female-only facilities work best for Berdu . . . [*Singing tunelessly*] . . . 'Berdu fahra' . . . who can tell me what Berdu fahra means?

Quatro 6 Dawn Berdu fah*ri* is Island of the future, brother. It's a reference to native knowledge, to the Island's traditional Yothi farming methods, and / to

[**Flick as lights black out.* **The Examiner** *can be heard huffing and puffing outside*]

Mono 14 Anita Another goddam black out

Mono 15 Matty Um . . . is someone at the gate?

[****Master of Discipline** *rushes to punch in the entry code*]

*Gates open

Enter the **Examiner***, wearing an eccentric gold outfit and carrying a touch-screen tablet*

The Examiner [*panting*] . . . Whatta . . . top notch . . . establishment

Master of Discipline Welcome, Examiner!

The Examiner Hi there, Meathead. Christ, you look shit. Are those a new pair of glasses?

Master of Discipline I know the master code! I never forget! Number are colours! Six for blue!

The Examiner [*To* **Master**] . . . Try not to scream it to the heavens . . . [*To* **Trainees**] . . . You've all met my heavy?

Master of Discipline I never forget! I protect the Examiner! I am the Master!

The Examiner [*To* **Trainees**] . . . Master of the *single entendre*. I expect he's been waving his gun about?

Master of Discipline [*waving gun*] . . . I am the man with the gun! My gun has three bullets!

The Examiner Put it away now, Meathead

Instructor Glad you could make it, Examiner.

The Examiner . . . I'd much prefer you call me 'Dude.'

Assistant I like what you're wearing, Dude.

The Examiner Thanks Assistant. Yes, us geezers look great in gold, that's why I suggested it for Team Smile. Quite the superhero vibe. Hoo ha! I had a hand in these lovely little beaming logos also. And I'm pretty chuffed with how these trainee outfits all worked out. I did the moodboards you know. Blacks for Quatros, white for Monos . . .

Vice Examiner Classic!

Assistant [*beep] . . . If only to see your stunning outfit properly, I've beeped base to activate the generator

The Examiner Wow you are a suck up, Assistant! I'm going to call you Toady! . . . Unless it offends, Toady?

Assistant Not at all, Dude

Instructor [*beep . . . reading his tablet] . . . Sir, I have just received screen notification regarding Quatro 8.

The Examiner You mean we're a filly down?

Instructor It would mean a lot if you could hold the exam until I've collected her from her special assessment.

The Examiner If Special Quatro 8 is happy, the Dude is happy!

Instructor [*jangle of keys] . . . I appreciate that.

    [***Master of Discipline** dashes to punch in entry code]

           *Gate opens

                 [*Exit* **Instructor**

The Examiner While we wait, a few words about?

                 [*Gate closes

Vice Examiner . . . You?

The Examiner If you insist, Vice.

Vice Examiner The Dude is a ground-breaking expert in interconnectedness. He has passionately championed the link between positive language and behaviour. He has pioneered a way of completely controlling and dominating negativity. He designed the high-tech electric masks you're wearing, shortly to go global.

The Examiner [*flick as lights are turned on*] . . . Light at last! I'll take it from here, Vice! Girlies, the point of the mask is to prevent you from saying . . . shall I demonstrate? [*Feigns suffering*] . . . 'No!' 'No!!!' 'No?' . . . Why aren't I getting shocked, Vice?

Vice Examiner You're er . . . not wearing a Smile?

The Examiner 'Master, care to demonstrate . . . as per? . . . 'no'? . . . [*Silence*] . . . Perhaps later . . . [*Chortles*] . . . now then, who can tell me something I want to hear?

Vice Examiner *I* have some *uplifting* news, Dude. The Report-a-Frown figures for last quarter are so high that unit capacity will rise to ten.

Quatro 6 Dawn Wait . . . but there's only four mattresses?

Quatro 7 Rosie We ain't kipping with *ones, bro*?!

Vice Examiner Increasing capacity is excellent for Smile's income generation?

The Examiner Well why didn't you say?

Quatro 9 Paula [*concerned*] . . . Beware overcrowding, brother.

The Examiner . . . Look lively now girlies

Quatro 6 Dawn Wait . . . but . . . ?

The Examiner Tannoy, Countdown!

[*The theme tune from* Countdown *plays*]

The Examiner Question one!   What is Smile's primary line of business?

Vice Examiner Excuse me, is this the exam?

Master of Discipline This is not the exam!

Quatro 7 Rosie . . . Surveillance!

The Examiner [*feigning shock*] . . . Pardon!

Mono 16 Alex Smiles! Quality accessories!

The Examiner Phew! . . . Question two! Besides making female face-wear, what gainful employment do we offer this Island's men?

Master of Discipline Shooting and killing!

The Examiner Shut up, Meathead!

Mono 15 Matty Um . . . Protection! Enrolment in Protection!

The Examiner Right on the money! Question three! What's the third Smile on the male menu?

Quatro 6 Dawn Um . . . Drilling?

Vice Examiner Smile prefers to say . . .

Mono 14 Anita . . . *Extraction*? To s*upport* income generation?

The Examiner Hoo ha! And the fourth string to Smile's bow?

Quatro 9 Paula Prisons, brother?

The Examiner Bzzz!

Master of Discipline Positive language!

Quatro 9 Paula '. . . Language Correction Centres'!

The Examiner Tannoy stop! . . . [*Music stops*] [*Yawns*] . . . What next?

Vice Examiner Perhaps . . . an evidence op?

The Examiner Like it, Vice! . . . Tannoy, 'Everything is awesome!'

[*Music can be heard* – Everything is awesome – *playing over the speakers*]

Mono 14 Anita Um . . . is *this* the exam?

Master of Discipline This is not the exam! Dance! Smile!

[*The* **Trainees** *dance. Half-blinded by the masks, they start to bump into each other*]

Mono 14 Anita [*as* **Rosie** *bumps into her*] . . . God . . . watchit . . . get off!

Quatro 7 Rosie You gerroff!

Mono 16 Alex [*lowered voice*] . . . These farm hands stink

Quatro 9 Paula [*lowered voice*] . . . ponces

Mono 14 Anita [*lowered voice*] . . . scum

The Examiner And some thumbs-up to the camera, you left-footed Staceys? [*The* **Trainees** *give thumbs up*] . . . Like it! Did anyone say like it?

Master of Discipline Like it!

Mono 16 Alex Like it, darling!

Mono 15 Matty Um . . . like it?

Mono 14 Anita Like it!

The Examiner I can't hear you, Quatros?

Quatro 6 Dawn Wait . . . but . . . Like it?

[**Beep. Flash of camera*]

[*Music offstage*]

Automated tannoy sound effect Evidence captured!

[**Jangle of* **Instructor**'s *keys from outside*]

Gates unlock

Enter **Instructor** *with* **Quatro 8 Beth** [*wearing regulation black*] *and* **Mono 2 Ray** [*wearing regulation white*] *both masked*

The Examiner Well, well, well. Look what the cat dragged in.

The Examiner Mono . . . [**Beep*] . . . read from display!

[**Gates locked*

Mono 2 Ray [*reading from display, working class*] . . . 'Mono 2: Bad mental health'

The Examiner Bzzz! This bitch is a lifer. I evidenced her myself.

Mono 2 Ray I corrected.

The Examiner What?

Mono 2 Ray I corrected your 'evidence.' My correction was validated?

[**The Examiner** *is temporarily wrongfooted*]

Instructor Dude, Mono 2 is due out tomorrow. Her entire floor has been relocated. Water on the light fittings. She'll be in with us too. And this is Quatro 8, whose reading has just been assessed.

Master of Discipline Quatro . . . [**Beep*] . . . read your error!

Quatro 8 Beth . . . Sir, could you . . . [*Whispering*] . . . duri?

The Examiner [*angry*] . . . Crazies and imbeciles, the lot of you . . . Tannoy, 'Countdown'!

[**The theme tune from* Countdown *can be heard*]

Quatro 8 Beth [*increasingly anxious*] . . . Brother . . . [*Whispering*] . . . duri?

Instructor Dude, Quatro 8 is dyslexic.

The Examiner . . . You mean you haven't corrected that?

Quatro 8 Beth It's . . . [*whispering*] gali?

The Examiner What's wrong with her? Why's she whispering 'dubdebub'?

Quatro 9 Paula She sings when she's worried, brother?

The Examiner [*patronizing*] . . . Poor little love . . . One little sentence, Special . . . It's on the screen there! . . . Take your time . . . you can do it?

[*The theme tune from* Countdown *continues playing on a loop*]

Quatro 8 Beth [*staring at display screen*] . . . 'Quatro 8' . . .

The Examiner Very good?

Quatro 8 Beth 'Fer' . . . um . . . 'fath' . . .

The Examiner What was that?

Quatro 8 Beth . . . 'Fayo' . . . 'Fagfer' . . .

The Examiner [*as* **Assistant** *giggles nervously*] . . . Tannoy, stop! [**Countdown theme tune stops*] Sadly there appears to be something uncorrectable about this illiterate young Quatro, whose inability to manage language / is

Mono 2 Ray Not a fucking crime!

Vice Examiner On the contrary, how we speak shapes how we act. Refusing to speak at the appropriate time in the appropriate way constitutes a threat to all Smile stands for.

The Examiner In life there are winners and losers. Special, who do you identify with?

Quatro 8 Beth . . . I'm a loser.

Instructor Er, just a moment. Quatro 8 has already completed her reading test. Regarding the actual exam, it's only fair she take it with the others?

Quatro 8 Beth It's alright . . . [*Depressed,* **Beth** *lies down on a mattress*] . . . I'm tired.

The Examiner Glad we're all happy. Tannoy, 'Happy'!

[**Music can be heard*: Happy *by Pharrell Williams*]

Master of Discipline Trainees, impersonate each other! Quatro 7, go!

Quatro 6 Dawn Wait . . . but?

Master of Discipline This is the exam! Trainees, impersonate each other! Quatro 7, go!

Quatro 7 Rosie 'Wait . . . but?'

The Examiner What?

Master of Discipline This is the exam!

Quatro 7 Rosie 'Wait . . . but?' . . . I'm her, I'm Quatro 6?

The Examiner Let's shake this up. Quatros act Monos, Monos Quatros!

Quatro 6 Dawn Wait . . . but?

Quatro 9 Paula [*lowered voice*] . . . Act Mono? Put on an accent?

Quatro 6 Dawn [*unconvincing posh accent*] ' . . . Poor me! . . . I'm a poor little rich girl! . . . Daddy runs the government! . . . I'm a daddy's girl!'

Mono 15 Matty Um . . . I don't get it?

Quatro 22 Cat She's being me, sister.

The Examiner Give us a twirl, gals! [**The Examiner** *dances with* **Quatro 6 Dawn** *and* **Quatro 9 Paula**]

Quatro 22 Cat [*lowered voice*] . . . Sisters, I want you to know that I never took my father's money . . . I protested this facility, their extraction program, their bankrolling of the army . . . all of it

Quatro 7 Rosie [*lowered voice*] . . . Yeah right

Master of Discipline Mono 15, go!

Mono 15 Matty [*unconvincing working-class accent*] . . . 'I'm a lifer, I'm like . . . really bad'

Mono 2 Ray [*sitting down on* **Beth***'s mattress*] . . . That's it, I'm out

Master of Discipline Quatro 22, go!

Quatro 22 Cat I do not wish to mock anyone. I'm out too, brother. And I call on my sisters to also abstain?

Quatro 7 Rosie [*lowered voice*] . . . They must love her on their poncy marches . . .

Master of Discipline Quatro 7, go!

Quatro 7 Rosie [*unconvincing posh accent*] '. . . My parents are rich . . . I love getting backhanders! . . . and being loaded'!

Quatro 9 Paula [*unconvincing posh accent*] '. . . I rarely stay here . . . uncle left me the place . . . for my property portfolio!'

Quatro 6 Dawn [*unconvincing posh accent*] '. . . Darling Mumsy pulled some strings to get me out! Cheers for the fast-track, Ma!'

Quatro 7 Rosie [*unconvincing posh accent*] '. . . Exxon paid for our palace! Shell headhunted Dad! He's their first Green Exec! I'm so proud! I want to be just like pops!'

Quatro 9 Paula 'I'm from nowhere! . . . I'm scared of plants! . . . I think milk's *manufactured!*'

Quatro 6 Dawn 'I'm trendy! . . . I'm an activist! . . . A fancy, activist Mono! . . . I protest . . . cause I'm fancy'!

Quatro 7 Rosie Rich bitch Monos!

Mono 16 Alex Quatro fucking rubes!

The Examiner [*amused*] '. . . Rubes'

Mono 14 Anita [*unconvincing working-class accent*] '. . . I never climb a tree or stage a sit-in . . . I never do anything brave like that!'

Mono 16 Alex [*unconvincing working-class accent*] '. . . I just pick fruit, get high . . . and sing!'

Quatro 7 Rosie Enjoy your 'holiday house,' princess?

Mono 16 Alex Jealous, peasants?

Quatro 6 Dawn These c***s suck government dick!

Quatro 9 Paula [*sarcastic, 'posh'*] '. . . Your spreadsheets are delicious!'

Quatro 7 Rosie [*sarcastic, 'posh'*] '. . . Your budgets make me wet!'

Quatro 6 Dawn [*sarcastic, 'posh'*] '. . . Yummy!'

Quatro 9 Paula Champagne 'activists'!

Quatro 7 Rosie Eco-fucking-toffs!

Quatro 6 Dawn No clue how to plant, or reap, or sow!

Quatro 9 Paula Killing kandril!

Quatro 6 Dawn Crushing coshu, spraying yangle!

Quatro 9 Paula Selling history! Selling kinla!

Quatro 6 Dawn Getting rich off our freela!

Mono 16 Alex Stupid lying ugly inbreds!

Mono 14 Anita Lazy druggy Quatro crims!

Mono 15 Matty What kind of mum leaves their kid for *four years*?!

Quatro 6 Dawn [*lowered voice*] . . . Shut up . . . [*Louder*] . . . Shut up!

Vice Examiner Oh dear.

[***The Examiner** turns music off*]

[*Drip continues*]

The Examiner Supremely positive lingo, Monos! All except that lifer there, obviously. The rest of you, behind the desk! Congrats, winners!

Quatro 6 Dawn Wait . . . but what about us?

[**Mono 14 Anita**, **Mono 15 Matty** *and* **Mono 16 Alex** *move behind the desk with the staff*]

The Examiner Quatros, that was a spectacularly depressing performance. Luckily for you, the Dude is a softy. The jury's still out. Monos, I need your help here. How to make them up their game?

Mono 16 Alex You could shock them, darling?

The Examiner That might be a bit much at this stage. Nowhere to go really after that. Any other brainwaves?

Mono 14 Anita Make them empty their pockets? [*Pointing at* **Dawn**] . . . there's a bulge there

The Examiner Well well well! Brownie points for Mono 14!

Quatro 6 Dawn [*lowered voice*] . . . Oh god . . .

The Examiner [*pointing at her pocket*] . . . Empty your pockets you dishonest, thieving four!

Quatro 6 Dawn [*handing over the marble*] . . . I found it on the beach . . . under a sandbag . . . I wanted to . . . [*Getting emotional*] . . . give my boy something

The Examiner . . . On the mattress, loser!

[*Drip continues*]

Instructor Sir regarding negativity, please bear in mind that it has been a tough day for Quatros. As you know, the beach where our trainees do Duty is where the Island woman's / funeral

The Examiner The 'instructor' disguised as a bloke? I killed that imposter bitch myself!

Instructor [*as* **Assistant** *bursts into nervous laughter*] . . . I didn't know that . . . My point is, I know these women. I know that they embody a kind of passion that is both highly positive and extremely particular to Coraim Berdu. Quatro 6, for example, is truly of the earth – a wonderful mother who must be allowed to return to her son. Quatro 9 is exceptionally gifted. She is like water; a true seer, visions run through her, I've seen it. / Quatro

The Examiner Are you *gay?*

Instructor If I could just finish? Quatro 7 has the power of wind, of air – her desire to break free utterly irrepressible.

The Examiner [*amused*] . . . And the Special wet blanket?

Instructor Quatro 8 deserves to evidence herself . . . [*To* **Quatro 9 Paula**] . . . Quatro 9, if you could please just er…?

Quatro 9 Paula [*to* **Beth**] [*lowered voice*] . . . Sister, wake up . . . [*As* **Beth** *rubs eyes*] . . . it's your exam?

[**Beth** *stands*]

Instructor [*aside*] . . . Quatro 22, hit my playlist?

Quatro 22 Cat [*aside*] . . . Sure

Instructor [*aside*] . . . Just play along. Don't be afraid to show your true colours. You can do this, Beth

Quatro 22 Cat [*aside*] . . . Ready?

[**Music can be heard* – Lilac Wine *by Nina Simone* – *playing from one minute in*]

Instructor [*turning to* **Beth**] . . . Sister?

Quatro 8 Beth Ye? . . . I mean . . . [*Singing*] . . . 'yes'?

Instructor Sister I miss you. I remember the stories we used to make up, stories of demons and trolls. I hear the wind and it sounds like your voice, I hear it and I feel free

Quatro 8 Beth [*lowered voice*] . . . Sir . . . [*Singing*] . . . please?

Instructor Sister it was wrong. It was wrong what he did.

Quatro 8 Beth Sir, I . . .

The Examiner Do you mean to humiliate this poor girl?

Quatro 8 Beth . . . I . . . I [*Whispering*] . . . caina

Mono 2 Ray [*lowered voice*] . . . Babe, I got this . . .

[*Vision effect kicks in – the sound of the sea*]

Instructor Sister I feel you. I feel the rain in your eyes, the rumbling anger in your belly.

Mono 2 Ray I feel it too. I feel fire.

Instructor If this was a story I'd chant a spell and you'd appear. I would find you in a cave or a flower, magically safe and sound. Sometimes when I wake, I forget you've gone and try to keep sleeping. Sister, I want him to pay . . .

Mono 2 Ray He should pay

Instructor [*calm*] . . . It hurts, sister . . . It aches to my bones, unbearable . . . the rage in my hands, to my fingers . . . burning

Mono 2 Ray . . . burning

Master of Discipline No touching!

The Examiner [*turning the music off – vision effect off*] . . . have you lost your mind man?

Instructor Excuse me?

The Examiner Vice, take this lunatic's keys!

Instructor What? [*Jangling as he hands over keys*] . . . Here

The Examiner You are a pussy

Instructor With respect, my main concern is the release of these women. Quatro 8, I apologise if I put you on the spot there – I may have got slightly carried away. I was only trying to demonstrate that Quatro 8 is genuinely positive, like all my trainees. Examiner, I know for a fact that all my Quatros are all in the system, / and

The Examiner [*cheerful*] . . . Well why didn't you say?

Instructor So . . . you mean . . . so . . . they're all be released?

The Examiner [**beep*] . . . Check your screen, man . . .

Instructor [*reading*] . . . Another trainee?!

The Examiner Go fetch.

Instructor Right . . . the thing is, with all these leaks, the electrics are bound to spark somewhere . . . Sir you may not know it, but the gas is really quite close to this unit / and

The Examiner Go save that damsel!

Vice Examiner Safety first?!

[****Vice Examiner** *inserts entry code*]

*Gates open

[*Exit* **Instructor**

[**Gates close*

The Examiner . . . Now the old worry wort's out the way . . . waddaya say we get those masks *off*, ladies?

[*With a series of *click-click-clicks the* **Vice Examiner** *starts unlocking the* **Trainees'** *masks*]

Mono 16 Alex . . . Cheers, darling.

Mono 14 Anita God that's better

The Examiner I'm a liberal, aren't I Vice?

Vice Examiner . . . Smile believes that everyone is free . . . [*Click*] . . . The masks are optional . . . Within this facility, we simply recommend them, / when

The Examiner Not the rabid whore! Not old horse face! She may wear lily white, but leave that muzzle on! . . . Now then, what's four minus three ones?

Assistant One . . .

The Examiner One more seat on the freedom train!

Mono 15 Matty [*lowered voice*] . . . Um . . . I'm confused?

The Examiner By the maths, sweet cakes?

Mono 2 Ray By your fucking efforts to screw us over!

The Examiner Tell them, Meathead! . . . [*Beep*] . . . As beeped, birdbrain? Everything is beeped? Check your screen, beep-head!

Master of Discipline [*checking his beeper*] . . . New quotas! Only four trainees will be released! [*Gasps from* **Trainees**]

*Rattling from outside

Instructor Could you er . . . open the gate for us?

*****Master of Discipline** *punches in entry code*

*Gates open

Enter **Instructor**
with **Mono 8 Rachel***, who wears white and a mask*

Vice Examiner [*tepid*] . . . That was quick.

[**Gates close*

Instructor As luck would have it, Mono 8 here was only two floors down.

Mono 8 Rachel [*well-spoken*] . . . Paula? . . . Pauls, man! It's Rach! [*Lowered voice*] . . . Your mum was my nanny? You're out tomorrow too?

The Examiner Welcome, sweetie pie! As you can see, these ug pugs are down in the mouth . . . [*Click as **Master of Discipline** *unlocks mask*] . . . you're just the pretty, cheerful soul we need!

Instructor Mono 8 passed her test last week. As her unit is undergoing emergency rewiring, she will be in with us also. Since all Trainees' release day is tomorrow, I think just this once we'll take the risk.

[**Vice Examiner** *and* **The Examiner** *chortle*]

Instructor Why are you laughing?

The Examiner Completely out of my hands. Very upsetting.

Instructor You don't look very upset.

The Examiner [*cheerful*] '. . . Sad face.'

Instructor You're smiling.

Assistant [*beep] . . . Dude, I've just beeped you the info regarding Mono 8.

The Examiner [*reading tablet*] . . . That bad apple? Bad luck, sugarplum. We incidented him yesterday, invalidated all his validations – total nightmare, administratively

Mono 8 Rachel I don't understand . . .

The Examiner Not to worry, you can just take your chances with these girls

Mono 8 Rachel . . . And what are my chances?

The Examiner . . . I don't think it would be fair to speculate . . .

Mono 16 Alex [*as* **Mono 8 Rachel** *heads for the mattresses*] . . . Sit with us darling, you're not a four.

Mono 8 Rachel . . . I'll sit with my friend, thanks.

Instructor Examiner, what happened after you sent me to collect Mono 8?

The Examiner It's slipped my mind

Master of Discipline New quota! As beeped! You beeped me the quota! New quota is four!

Instructor [*shocked*] . . . are you making this up?

The Examiner Do you think I got where I am by *lying*?

Vice Examiner The Examiner has been very honest about the statistics. The girls on the mattress have a one-in-seven chance of success.

The Examiner Sounds about right. Where were we, Mono 16?

Mono 16 Alex As I recall, darling, you did ask the thieving fours to empty their pockets and confess?

The Examiner So I did!

Instructor But . . . but this is monstrous . . .

The Examiner Is it? Four girls will be released, I promise. That's better than nothing.

Master of Disciple You're not a monster!

The Examiner I wonder. I worry that slaving away here may have . . . dried me out. Let's find out. Let's get the juices flowing. To pass that fourth lucky broad, I'll need a confession that *makes me cry*.

Vice Examiner [*concerned*] . . . could you repeat that?

The Examiner 'Make me cry!'

[** The camera flashes*]

Automated tannoy sound effect Evidence captured.

[**Quatros** *turn out their pockets. All except* **Paula**'s *are empty*]

Vice Examiner I must have misunderstood . . . [*Confused*] . . . you can't intend to incite negativity?

The Examiner Well, well, well! What have we here?

Quatro 9 Paula [*handing over a long, fat roll up*] . . . It grows wild all over the Island . . . I gather it while on Duty

The Examiner [*sniffing*] . . . Yangle! . . . [**Sparking up*] . . . Quatro 9, you're on!

Instructor Ready?

[The **Instructor** *turns on music*: Another Lonely Day *by Ben Harper*]

Quatro 9 Paula I confess to smoking yangle. When I smoke it, I have visions. My vision is flames . . . Flames of your furies, red at our gate. Flames of my sisters' passion, that lives forever

Instructor Quatro 9, you're burning up?

Mono 8 Rachel . . . She might cool down if she wore her vest?

Assistant Grey vests *are* regulation?

The Examiner [*cheerful*] . . . Bzzz! There goes your promotion, Toads! Black for Quatro, white for Mono, my design is textbook! [*Amused*] . . . if they're not ripping each other apart, how will we keep the bitches down? [**Paula** *takes her top off, revealing regulation grey vest*] . . . Then again . . . if the girl wants to strip, who am I to refuse? [*Wolf whistles*]

Quatro 22 Cat Ignore him, sister

Mono 14 Anita [*concerned*] . . . Is she alright?

Quatro 6 Dawn [*reassuring*] . . . She will be. She always rides it out

Quatro 9 Paula Berdu's spirit is strong. Hollow her out at your peril, she will respond.

The Examiner . . . Excuse me . . . [*Inhaling*] . . . Is your illegal herb supposed to make one . . . [*coughing*] . . . cough?

Quatro 9 Paula Your hate is death that chokes you, brother. Our Island's power . . . is life

The Examiner [*coughs*] . . . 'life'?

[**Vision effect kicks in – the sound of the sea*]

Quatro 9 Paula Life in our budding plants, bursting at the highest temperature. Life in my sisters' wombs, which open at the highest threshold of pain. Life in the flocks, the busy beehives . . . Life that will walk through your flames . . . to the awesome judgement . . . of thunder

[**With a crackle, music flicks off*]

Quatro 9 Paula [*seeming to see somebody no one else can*] . . . I see you

Mono 15 Matty . . . the music just switched itself off?

Quatro 9 Paula I see you, sister . . . When the poisoned land ruptures, I feel you bleed . . . when these walls flood, waters rise in your eyes . . . when our lights flicker, fires crackle in your belly . . . when we turn on each other, armies rage . . . /the cameras have drills . . . they're turning on us . . . I see red . . . I see red . . .

[**High pitched note fades out as* **Dawn** *begins to quietly sing over* **Paula**]

Quatro 6 Dawn [*to the tune of* Sing A Rainbow]

Wubbub Berdu sitar cree
Puidhe clinny a blee
Halarth clan ye im freel /
Coraim sicree ais seel

(*middle eight*)

Ye ah cloyais yaim ah fein
Ye ah grul ah grun a carm
Ah fla fumedd grunga hein
Ah soarliso, gree a barm

(*to the tune of the first verse*)
Creicor fahri sithin ye
Grandi golda eh see blee
Fanail dunsta ah hi fellair
Wubbub nee endair

The Examiner [*interrupting and talking over*] . . . I've heard
this 'bubtiwubtub' before . . . We're drilling away, we're
hitting the good stuff . . . some Island bitch rocks up,
right Meathead? . . . Starts bloody chanting! . . . Says the
land's fucking 'sacred'! . . . [*Breathless*] . . . Meathead, you
buttoned this collar too tight . . . 'Bodies and burials' . . .
I looked it up! . . . / . . . it's your fucking . . . [*Breathing
faster*] . . . death song! . . . [*Hyperventilating*] . . . I know
your curses, witches! . . . I can't breathe! . . . I ca – . . .

[**The Examiner** *heaves with loud, panicked, dry-eyed sobs.*
**Flash of camera. Sound of the sea stops*]

Automated tannoy sound effect Evidence captured!

[***The Examiner** *passes out with a thud*]

Master of Discipline [*to tablet*] . . . Code crash! Code
crash! Vice! Assistant! Operation reboot! Follow me! . . .
[*Entering code] . . . I, I never forget! . . . [*Rattling*] Numbers
are colours! . . . [*Re-entering] . . . Six for blue, / then

Vice Examiner Oh for God's sake

[***Vice Examiner** *inputs the entry code*]

*Gates open

[*Exit* **Vice Examiner**, **Master of Discipline** *and* **Assistant**

[*Gates close

[**The Examiner** *gives a grunt and rolls over*]

Quatro 7 Rosie [*disappointed*] . . . And the bastard's still
breathing . . .

Mono 2 Ray Still, they got him sobbing on camera. You deserve to get out for that, babe.

Quatro 9 Paula Thank you, sister

Instructor [*covering the camera with his jacket*] . . . Now we're alone, I'll just cover that camera . . . [*Bringing out wine and cups*] . . . A little coshu wine?

Mono 15 Matty I'd kill for some water.

Mono 16 Alex I'm famished, darling.

Quatro 7 Rosie Ain't in the party mood, bro

Instructor I quite understand. On behalf of those who did not pass, I shall be notifying base of how poorly the Examiner treated you.

Mono 2 Ray We should correct the evidence. It worked for me, got me down to Mono. They all saw him shoot that lady, they might listen.

Quatro 9 Paula You're right, sister. As a soon as I'm out, I'll call for your release . . .

Mono 14 Anita Is your friend still asleep?

Mono 8 Rachel [*to* **Paula**] . . . Will you call for my release, Pauls?

Mono 14 Anita I'm not being funny, but has she taken something?

Mono 8 Rachel [*sad*] . . . Why won't you look at me, Pauls?

Quatro 9 Paula [*fond*] . . . Oh Rach . . . [*Sad*] Some things, it hurts to see . . . I knew your colours wouldn't change . . . I see the girl in you, in us . . . [*With growing conviction*] . . . You taught me to swim in the rock pools . . . you held my hand in the dark . . . When I hid from the ghosts no one else could hear, you brought coshu and water to the forest . . . When they called me a witch . . . when we were nine . . . the first time they called me a witch . . . [*Getting upset*] . . . it was you who . . .

Mono 8 Rachel [*with   sympathetic   recognition*] . . .   Oh
Pauls . . . You're here for your gift . . .

Quatro 9 Paula Where were you? I know we haven't kept
in touch, / but

Mono 8 Rachel [*apologetic*] . . . I should have been here.
I should have known. What did you see?

Quatro 9 Paula Greying sea urchins. Disintegrating star
fish. Green fleshed animals no yothi can eat. Crystal
streams thickening, slick, sludgy sickening. Brown water.
Barrenness. I told them years ago. They put me here.

Mono 14 Anita [*horrified*] . . . God are you serious? But
all that happened, they can't lock you up for *warning*
them? . . . Pass me a cup, I need a drink . . . What are
you lot in for?

Quatro 7 Rosie I'm in for sleeping rough

Quatro 6 Dawn My boy was starving – I stole some bread

Mono 14 Anita What about her?

Quatro 7 Rosie . . . They made her sign a confession . . .
she couldn't read it . . .

Mono 14 Anita Seriously, shouldn't we try and wake her?
If she's taken pills, it's important / we

Quatro 7 Rosie She should be so fucking lucky

Mono 15 Matty [*sympathetic*] . . . Let the poor thing sleep,
Neets . . . so you all got four years?

Mono 16 Alex [*shocked*] . . . that's awful, darlings . . .
Instructor, give these girls a drink.

[**Instructor** *distributes cups of wine*]

Mono 16 Alex [*lowered voice] . . . I thought they were
lazy, thieving druggies, Matts.

Mono 15 Matty [*lowered voice] . . . I called her a bad
mum.

Mono 14 Anita [*lowered voice*] . . . God Alex, I made out like her 'see the future' act was lies. [*Drinking stops*]

Mono 15 Matty Here, for your son . . . [*Emptying pocket*] . . . from the beach . . . My daughter loved them when she was little . . . The colours really. . . made her smile . . .

Mono 16 Alex Darling, I shouldn't have slagged you off.

Mono 14 Anita We shouldn't have doubted you. God, what you said . . . what you saw . . . you made the bastard pass out

Mono 2 Ray Too right . . . fuck, let's all get sloshed . . . [*Pouring*] . . . That dude's a walking panic attack, he knows his days are numbered! His drilling's toxic, he knows he's digging death, he knows Berdu will rise up, he knows it with every quake!

[*The ground starts to shake*]

The Examiner [*coming to*] Hoo ha!

Enter **Vice Examiner**, **Assistant** *and* **Master of Discipline**, *laden with snacks, which they drop*

The Examiner What the fuck are you doing! Get it together, man!

Vice Examiner The ground's, er . . . shaking?

[*Shaking stops*]

The Examiner Care to offer a starving man some grub?

Vice Examiner [*offering snacks*] . . . Sir, we brought a choice of snacks which historically have always revived you.

[*The Examiner* *eats noisily*]

Instructor [*dashing to remove his jacket from the camera*] . . . er, just a moment

Vice Examiner Instructor, what's going on?

Instructor Bit chilly . . . thought I'd put my jacket on?

The Examiner [*eating noisily*] Vice, why are you looking at me like that?

Vice Examiner Glad to see you're no longer hyperventilating, dude . . . or crying . . .

The Examiner My eyes are always dry?

Vice Examiner . . . I'm referring to er . . . the evidence captured on camera?

Master of Discipline Camera captures negativity!

Assistant Correct me if I'm wrong, but negativity at the Dude's level hardly seems relevant

The Examiner Spot on, Toad

Vice Examiner It's more a matter of consistency?

The Examiner Are you suggesting I do not *define* the rules? I invented the exponential Smile algorithm! The unstoppable *force* behind all our fortunes!

Vice Examiner Gosh you certainly did! Dude, it's simply / that . . .

The Examiner That's Sir to you.

Vice Examiner I'll just quickly review the records . . .

The Examiner [**rewinding starts*] . . . Stop it! Stop that, Vice! . . . Toady, a Smile for this traitor!

Vice Examiner [*rewinding continues as the* **Assistant** *wrestles him into a mask*] . . . Hey . . . [**Click*] Get off me! . . . [*Shock*] . . . ow . . . [*Shock*] . . . ah!

The Examiner [**rewinding stops*] . . . Are you suggesting I'm a monster?

Vice Examiner You're not a monster! Please! Stop the shocks!

The Examiner Um, what's the word I'm looking for? The word we can say but they can't?

[**The Examiner** *and* **Assistant** *chortle*]

The Examiner [**ringing to touch-screen*] . . . Base, traitor incidented . . .

    [**The* **Master of Discipline** *punches in entry code*]

        *Gates unlocked

Automated tannoy sound effect Preparing to shoot the traitor!

        [*Exit* **Vice Examiner**

Assistant Bye bye Vice!

        [**Gates locked*

Assistant Don't you worry, Sir – that's the last we'll see of him.

[*Silence*]

The Examiner . . . You missed a button, Instructor.

Instructor What?

The Examiner When you stuffed on your jacket, the jacket covering the camera? You missed a button.

Instructor Oh. Right . . . [*Rebuttoning his jacket*] . . . I think the women are entitled to some privacy.

The Examiner [*sly*] . . . you've been getting jiggy with the fours!

Instructor That's obscene . . . please show my trainees some respect.

The Examiner You really are an 'Island woman'

Instructor Thank you.

The Examiner It wasn't a compliment, thicko!

Instructor I was always taught to look up to women . . . My father worshipped my mother . . . like the sun . . . [*Reminiscing*] . . . like looking at her . . . blinded him . . . He looked at my sister, my older sister . . . like something he could never have imagined . . . he looked at her . . . like she was the most precious thing

The Examiner I'm afraid the incest testimonials won't wash. Now if these nice sophisticated Monos had objected to the camera, I might have asked the old Master to shoot it / but

Instructor What does my trainees being Quatro have to do with it?

Master of Discipline Fours are negative! Fours are islanders!

Instructor Examiner, you know that's not true. Coraim Berdu has always welcomed everyone. Quatro 6 only moved here after her / marriage

Mono 8 Rachel I'm an Islander and I'm a one?

The Examiner You enunciate, darling?

Mono 2 Ray 'Enunciate' this – 'I'm mono, mate!'

Quatro 22 Cat I'm Quatro, brother?

The Examiner Because you're bad! Fours are bad!

Instructor Examiner, you're rude and you make no sense.

The Examiner If you can't grasp the difference between good and bad, you're really not Smile material! You'll be farming with spoons and singing berdiwubwub next!

Instructor We do sing it. [*Singing*] . . . 'Wubbub Berdu sitar cree' . . . [*Stops singing*] . . . 'beloved berdu sister true' . . . It's the island mourning song. We sang it today.

The Examiner Not here you didn't.

Instructor We sang it at the funeral. On the beach.

The Examiner 'We?'

Instructor The woman you shot . . . was my sister.

[*Gasps from the* **Trainees**]

[**Drip continues*]

The Examiner Well, well, well. Good job we took those keys. No wonder you fucked with surveillance. No wonder these crims regret nothing.

Mono 2 Ray [*calm*] . . . I regret

The Examiner [*delighted*] . . . Horsey! Begging to be broken at last?

Mono 2 Ray [*calm*] . . . I regret not having stabbed your eyes out.

[**Drip continues*]

The Examiner You've obviously been brainwashed. You loved every second.

Mono 2 Ray You know what I said.

The Examiner I blame your instructor. Negativity is highly infectious. Group discipline it is . . . Where's that 'man with a gun'?

Master of Discipline [**gun cocked*] . . . Dude, I am pointing at each head in turn!

The Examiner Yes I'm not blind. I was actually revisiting that idea of yours, Mono 16, about the shocks?

Mono 16 Alex I actually meant . . . for the Quatros, darling?

The Examiner That's not really how the 'group' thing works. Unless old Horsey decides to fess / up?

Mono 2 Ray I'm always happy to set the record straight. The fact is . . .

Quatro 6 Dawn Don't say it, sister

Mono 15 Matty [*lowered voice*] . . . Please don't

Mono 2 Ray The fact is . . . I said no . . . [*Shock*]

[**Drip continues*]

The Examiner Meathead?

Mono 2 Ray [**gun cocked, defiant*] . . . No! . . . [*Shock*]

[**Lights flick off*]

[*In the dark, some glass shatters*]

[*The* **Master of Discipline** *wails with pain*]

[**Lights flick on*]

[**Ray**'s *arm is raised protectively to hide her face. The* **Master of Discipline** *clutches his bleeding eyes*]

Master of Discipline [*in pain*] . . . Turn the lights on!

Quatro 6 Dawn [*lowered voice*] . . . They are on?

Mono 2 Ray [*devastated*] . . . Oh my God . . . Oh my God . . .

Master of Discipline [*whimpering*] . . . I can't see . . .

[**The camera flashes*]

Automated tannoy sound effect Evidence captured!

The Examiner [*ripping bedclothes, using strips to bandage* **Master**'s *eyes*] . . . The records will show that Meathead incited negativity by baiting this crazy female to violence – his broken glasses and bleeding eyes prove his crime.

Instructor Sir, we saw you order / him

Master of Discipline [*increasingly muffled as* **The Examiner** *gags him*] . . . s-s-sor . . . s-s-s-sorry . . . p – p-please . . . w-w-wubbub . . . w-wubbub nee endi!

The Examiner [*still kicking*] . . . wubneefuck?

Master of Discipline I love you! [*Muffled cries as* **The Examiner** *gags* **Master of Discipline** *with bedclothes*]

Quatro 9 Paula 'What survives . . . is love'

Instructor The records will show that the Examiner has gagged his Master for following orders!

[*The camera flashes*]

Automated tannoy sound effect Evidence captured!

[**Master of Discipline** *sits on a mattress, gagged and shocked*]

The Examiner . . . Smiles for all I think, Toads?

Assistant Of course . . . I'll just click them on.

[**Assistant** *clicks masks on*]

Mono 16 Alex [*kicking* **Ray**, *click*] . . . Did the feminazi really stab his eyes out?

Mono 2 Ray [*getting kicked,* *click*] . . . I couldn't see . . .

Quatro 7 Rosie [*kicking* **Ray**, *click*] . . . Fucking psycho!

Instructor [*positioning himself so that the kicking stops*] . . . Ladies, stop kicking her!

Mono 2 Ray [*regaining her breath*] . . . It was an accident . . .

Instructor [*as* **Ray** *quietly weeps, unlocking her mask –* *click*] . . . I believe you

Assistant Instructor, relock Mono 2's Smile!

Instructor No.

The Examiner [*amused*] . . . As a Smile employee, I assure you he means 'yes.'

Instructor I mean no. She was crying. It hurts to cry beneath a mask.

The Examiner My eyes are always dry

Instructor So you've said. You've never grieved, or loved.

The Examiner Toady?

Assistant Smile! Support! Say yes!

Instructor Mono 2, 'say yes' to me chucking your 'beautiful, expensive Smile' in the bucket?

Mono 2 Ray 'Yes.'

The Examiner [The **Instructor** *drops* **Ray**'s *mask in the bucket – *fizz*] . . . Ridiculous.

Instructor The future always looks ridiculous.

The Examiner [*slow clapping his applause*] . . . If you want to destroy company property, it's your pay cheque, buddy . . . [*Pretending to be relaxed*] . . . if you want to throw electrical appliances into fucking water and risk everyone's safety, it's a free country.

Instructor Yes we're all 'free,' masks are 'optional,' . . . 'safety first.' What's been your experience of this 'correction facility' Quatro 9?

[*Vision effect – sound of the sea*]

Quatro 9 Paula [*as if possessed*] . . . Smile! . . . Fire! . . . Run! . . . [*Struggling to see something others can't*] . . . When Dudes applaud, little children die . . . [*Very calm*] . . . If they laugh, we should protest . . . If they say stay, we should go.

[*Silence – sound of the sea stops*]

The Examiner . . . Do you regret the wilful incitement of such propaganda, Instructor?

Instructor 'The evidence speaks for itself.' Urging trainees to make you cry, commanding the Master to violence; gagging him – over and over you break your own rules. Your negativity has been well documented by the camera.

The Examiner Thanks for the 'evidence' of your '*instruction*' . . . You can all bond further during lifelong correction!

Mono 16 Alex [*shocked*] . . . we're fucked, darlings

Mono 15 Matty [*worried*] . . . Um . . . but us lot passed?

Mono 14 Anita You passed us Monos!

The Examiner Yes old Ejit's really let you down.

Mono 16 Alex Fuck the Instructor! [*Kicking the* **Instructor**] Fuck you!

Quatro 22 Cat Stop it, sisters!

Mono 14 Anita [*kicking* **Instructor**] . . . Fuck him up, Dude!

The Examiner Certainly . . . Toads, lock on his Smile, and make it shocking.

Assistant [**click as mask locked on*] . . . Instructor, do you confess that your negativity has risked Coraim Berdu's future and these trainees' freedom?

Instructor No . . . [*Shock*] . . . I confess that our imprisonment has made you rich! . . . I confess that I say no! . . . [*Shock*] . . . to your Smile, to your masks! No . . . [*Shock*] . . . to flattening us like plastic . . . no . . . [*Shock*] . . . to making us all the same . . . no . . . [*Shock*] . . . to throwing us away! . . . to extracting and deadening us! . . . to your sick sadism . . . to your murder of hope, and beauty . . . and life

The Examiner Increate the voltage!

Instructor [*electric shock extremely loud, in pain*] . . . my sister . . . was pregnant!

[*Silence*]

Instructor [*panting*] . . . You didn't know that . . . did you?

Assistant Sir . . . are you alright?

The Examiner [*weak*] . . . Perfectly.

Instructor Who's with me? . . . [*Rallying*] . . . Who's with me?

Mono 2 Ray I am!

The Examiner [*rallying*] Just you, Horsey?

Instructor Who else?

Mono 15 Matty Don't trust him! He's a man! He's on their payroll!

Mono 14 Anita Get away from him! Get off that mattress!

Instructor [*gentle*] . . . Sisters, I swear – I'm here to make a difference

Mono 16 Alex How's that working out for you, darling?

Mono 2 Ray Oh wake up!

Mono 14 Anita She fancies him!

Mono 2 Ray Men ain't generally my bag, but I know when to make an exception! This bloke stood up for us! Wears a fucking *mask* for us! You'd shit on your ally for lacking a cunt?

[** The **Instructor** turns on music*: Chain Reaction *by Diana Ross*]

The Examiner [*mocking*] *More* rabble rousing.

Instructor Glad my playlist is to your liking.

Quatro 22 Cat Sister, brother, I stand with you. I too have been kicked by the Islanders I love most. But like you, I never gave up on Berdu – the land of the future, the land of love. Don't we all have brothers or sons that we love? Like this man loves his sister?

Mono 16 Alex I'm here for my brother. He worked hard to buy his land. They shot him and left him to die in his own ditch.

Mono 8 Rachel I'm here for the man I love. He lost a hand in the mask factory. When we went to the press, they sewed his mouth shut. Compared to my boyfriend, I got off lightly.

Mono 14 Anita When they made my uncle give them his field, he knew he couldn't feed my cousins. He killed himself. That's why I protest. That's why I'm here.

Mono 15 Matty I'm here for my pothole campaign. My daughter fell twenty feet. She's crippled.

Quatro 6 Dawn I didn't know. I thought . . .

Mono 16 Alex You thought cause we're 'foreign,' and say 'darling,' we haven't suffered?

Quatro 7 Rosie Like we ain't fucking suffered?

The Examiner Cat fight! Hoo ha!

Mono 8 Rachel Enough, man! We're all stuck here, we've all suffered. Who cares if we're ones or fours? Children know better. D'you think I even knew that I was 'posh' when I was seven, or noticed how Pauls spoke? We're not the problem! The problem's him!

The Examiner I'm beginning to find this man-hating offensive.

Mono 16 Alex . . . What's offensive, darling, is you. We followed all your rules, even when you changed them. We did everything right. We jumped through all your hoops, even sided against other women – and for what?

Quatro 22 Cat . . . He used you, sisters. As he used my father.

The Examiner Your father knew exactly what he was doing. He was well compensated. Any issues, you take them up with him!

Quatro 22 Cat My father was bribed and lied to, as we all were. Sisters, brothers, we let them take our freedom, make money from our freedom – why on earth did we believe they would ever give it back?

[**Master of Discipline**'s *muffled cries grow louder.* **Beth** *gets up from her mattress, takes her top off to stand in her grey vest like* **Paula**]

The Examiner . . . Special! what a fetching little vest. Feeling 'hot'?

Quatro 8 Beth I'm neither hot nor cold . . . I just prefer grey . . . I see I'm not alone.

[**Mono 8 Rachel** *and* **Quatro 22 Cat** *and* **Mono 2 Ray** *take their tops off*]

The Examiner [*to* **Paula**] . . . Look what you've started, witch. You're all witches. You've not been sleeping at all, have you, you evil little eavesdropper?

Quatro 8 Beth I'm wide awake, brother. There is a Berdu saying – 'barrin bin sey aug' – we must look the beast in the eye. Sisters, until we do, outside will remain no better than in here. Whether we make it out or not is not what matters. This isn't just about freedom . . . It's about what's right.

[**Master of Discipline** *starts unlocking masks* . . . **click, click, click* . . . *the* **Trainees** *gasp*]

The Examiner [**turning music off*] What the hell are you doing, meathead?

Instructor [**click – gasping*] Ah, it's nice to breathe . . .

The Examiner Toads, you handle this.

Assistant Master, according to regulations, Smiles remain locked.

The Examiner [*trying to make light*] . . . Put it away you nutter . . . [*laughing nervously*] You are having a laugh . . . [**dialling to touch-screen, laid back*] . . . Base, you'll never believe it . . . the Master's gone kray kray . . . unlocking all the Smiles . . . [*Amused*] . . . some back up, cheers . . . yeah, a few heavies . . . [*Surprised*] . . . what . . . [*Worried*] . . . what?! . . . but . . . but I . . . sorry, sir . . . understood . . . apologies . . . affirmative . . . yes of course . . . yes right away . . . [*Hangs up*]

[**Assistant***'s touch-screen starts to ring*]

The Examiner Don't answer that! . . . [*Lowered voice*] . . . shit . . . fuck

Automated tannoy sound effect Examiner, report to incident room!

Quatro 7 Rosie Bro, that's where traitors are shot

[*Silence*]

Mono 2 Ray [*removing the Master's gag*] . . . Let's get that gag off you . . . get you some air . . .

Master of Discipline [*breathing*] . . . Thanks . . .

Mono 2 Ray 'course, mate . . . You did the same for us . . . Master, I'm so sorry . . .

Master of Discipline I did it . . . I panicked . . . I smashed my glasses . . .

Mono 2 Ray [*relieved*] . . . It wasn't me?

[*Silence*]

The Examiner . . . What are you up to?

Master of Discipline . . . is that you, my love?

The Examiner [*shivering*] . . . darling, your hands are cold.

Master of Discipline [*touching* **The Examiner***'s face*] . . . I used to adore this . . . the way you feel . . . our secret . . . the curves and valleys of your face . . . [*as mask is locked on – *click*] . . . ready for that demonstration, my love?

The Examiner Ow . . . ah . . . not so hard, darling . . . stop pressing it . . . no . . . [*Shock*] . . . please, my darling . . . no! [*Shock*] . . . . . . NO! . . . [*Shock*] . . . GET IT OFF ME!

Mono 16 Alex 'Super comfy,' aren't they? You designed them that way, right? They're worth a lot, right Dude? 'Oh *no!*' . . . [**Fizz*] . . . I dropped mine!

Quatro 7 Rosie '*No!*,' mine fell in the bucket too! [**Fizz*] . . . Aren't you going to do anything? Not very macho, 'Examiner.'

Mono 2 Ray [*fizz*] . . . Is Dude shitting his pants?

Quatro 8 Beth [*fizz*] . . . Has he lost his tool?

Mono 14 Anita [*fizz*] . . . Has his shrivelled drill dropped off?

Automated tannoy sound effect Shoot the traitor!

The Examiner [*as* **Master** *passes gun to* **Ray**, *hollow laughter*] . . . Meathead, you can't give a bitch a gun . . .

[**Ray** *shoots the camera – *bang, glass shatters. *Gun cocked*]

The Examiner [*sly*] . . . blasting the camera? Not very smart, lifer. They'll be here soon

Mono 2 Ray To 'shoot the traitor'? That's your problem, mate

The Examiner Looking a bit shaky, Horsey, a bit . . . rabbit in the headlights . . . something you . . . 'regret?'

Mono 2 Ray You'll regret . . . you'll regret that you ever . . . that you . . . [*Becoming emotional*] . . . you . . .

The Examiner That I *what*, dear?

[**Drip continues*]

Quatro 22 Cat . . . Sister, this man is no brother

Mono 16 Alex He killed my brother

Mono 15 Matty Crippled my daughter

Quatro 6 Dawn Starved my son

Quatro 7 Rosie Punished me for being alive

Mono 8 Rachel Tortured my boyfriend

Mono 14 Anita Drove my uncle to suicide

Quatro 22 Cat Scapegoated my family

Quatro 8 Beth Set me up.

Instructor Killed my sister

Master of Discipline Shocked me and gagged me

Mono 2 Ray [*calm*] . . . You raped me.

[*Silence. Quietly,* **Quatro 22 Cat** *starts to sing – then* **Paula**, *then* **Beth** *and* **Dawn** *and* **Rachel** *join, gradually getting louder as the* **Examiner** *talks over them*]

Quatro 22 Cat [*to the tune of* Sing A Rainbow]

> Wubbub Berdu sitar cree
> Puidhe clinny a blee /
> Halarth clan ye im freel
> Coraim sicree ais seel

Quatro 9 Paula [*middle eight*]

> Ye ah cloyais yaim ah fein
> Ye ah grul ah grun a carm
> Ah fla fumedd grunga hein
> Ah soarliso, gree a barm

Quatro 8 Beth
Quatro 6 Dawn

Mono 8 Rachel [*to the tune of the first verse*]

> Creicor fahri sithin ye
> Grandi golda eh see blee
> Fanail dunsta ah hi fellair
> Wubbub nee endair

The Examiner Not this again . . . [*Irritated, speaking over the singing as vision effect starts and gradually crescendos – sound of the sea*] . . . Christ you bitches are like dogs with bones . . . [*Coughs*] . . . you make me cough . . . you thump the fucking blood in my veins . . . even from the ground I hear you . . . over the sodding drills . . . I'm not stupid . . . I know what I've done . . . I know what I dig . . . from the buried bowels . . . the bones I dig up . . . the bones I sell . . . the bones I burn . . . I know what haunts me . . . wherever I am . . . I know what I burn . . . is alive

Master of Discipline Shoot the traitor!

[*The **Trainees** *stop singing – sound of the sea stops*]

Mono 2 Ray Examiner, you look worried. P'raps it's the gun thing. Guns ain't really my style . . . I'm gonna leave this here . . . [*Sets the gun on the table*]

Mono 2 Ray [*calm, speaking over the singing*] . . . Examiner, quick question as the 'language specialist'?

The Examiner Go on?

Mono 2 Ray It's about the word 'love' . . . 'wubbub', as my mates would say . . . they say it a lot, on the island . . . now love ain't a shock word . . . love is positive . . . so why, when you hear it . . . why d'you look frightened? Why d'you look cross?

The Examiner [*angry*] . . . I'm not cross! I'm not fucking frightened! I'm fucking bored shitless, love! What you airheads always fail to appreciate is that I'm a real man! That wubbdedub love shit is for losers like you!

[**Beth** *grabs the gun*]

Quatro 8 Beth [*with conviction*] She's not. A loser! [*She grabs the gun*]

Quatro 7 Rosie [*aside*] Fuck . . . she's picking it up

The Examiner The little dunce makes a comeback . . . no *whispering*, Special?

Quatro 8 Beth [**gun cocked, calm*] . . . 'I'm the girl with the gun.'

Mono 2 Ray Just for the record . . . Is there something you 'real men' do believe in . . . something the opposite of love, perhaps . . . something you value above everything . . . above people . . . above the whole earth, even . . . at any cost?

The Examiner Profit! [**Beth** *shoots* **The Examiner**]

Mono 2 Ray [*shocked*] . . . Beth, babe . . .

[*Silence*]

Quatro 22 Cat Is he gone, sisters?

[**The Examiner** *groans as he dies*

Master of Discipline . . . The monster's dead . . .

[*Silence*]

[*Suddenly, the* **Assistant** *laughs*]

Assistant [*nervous*] . . . I was thinking, you know . . . you need a word for this . . . this extremely admirable . . . 'saying no' thing . . .? I was thinking 'resistance' maybe . . .? I was hoping, maybe . . . to join your Resistance?

Mono 2 Ray What the . . .?

Master of Discipline Shoot the traitor! One bullet left!

Mono 14 Anita Let the bloke have his say.

Mono 2 Ray Assistant, on behalf of the Resistance, I'd like to ask . . . what do *you* believe in?

Assistant . . . Um er . . . you win

Mono 2 Ray It ain't about 'winning,' mate

Assistant [*calm*] . . . No . . . no I get that . . .just . . . shoot me now please er . . . Beth, was it?

Quatro 8 Beth Is there nothing you believe in, brother?

Assistant [*tortured*] . . . Christ . . . Christ this is hard . . . my father's a lawyer . . . I love my father . . . [*Impassioned*] . . . I thought this job would be great . . . the thing is . . . [*Guilty*] . . . I'm not proud of this . . . I thought I was better than women . . . [*Getting upset*] . . . I'm not evil, or stupid . . . I just used to think . . . if you're here, you must deserve it? [*Quietly miserable*] . . . but when they shot her . . . [*To* **Instructor**] . . . when they shot your sister . . . when she took off her jacket, never flinched . . . when I saw her, really saw her, a woman . . . so brave, so beautiful . . . when I saw the curve of her belly . . . when they shot her . . . [*Silence*] . . . My insides died that day . . . [*Resigned*] . . . Oh I know nothing's fair . . . but I never wanted *this* . . . this place, this uniform . . . I can't live like this, I can't wear this jacket . . . now you know . . . [**Assistant** *removes uniform to reveal a woman's form*] . . . fire away . . .

[*Gasps from the* **Trainees**]

Mono 2 Ray What's your name, Assistant?

Assistant Alice.

[*Silence.* **Beth** *shoots the ground* – *bang]

Quatro 8 Beth The barrel's empty.

Mono 2 Ray Welcome to the Resistance, Alice. I'm Ray.

Instructor Josh. Master?

Master of Discipline Forgot . . . forgot to remember . . .
forgot to see . . . I want to see . . . what you see . . . I want

Quatro 9 Paula [*offering a roll up*] . . . Yangle, brother?

[**Quatro 22 Cat** *lights the roll up for the* **Master of Discipline**.
He inhales]

Master Thanks.

Quatro 7 Rosie Is there any of that wine left, bro?

Mono 16 Alex Pass us a Snickers, darling?

Mono 15 Matty Um . . . some crisps please?

Quatro 6 Dawn [*enjoying food*] . . . Wow

Mono 8 Rachel [*eating*] . . . Man that's good

Mono 14 Anita . . . Could I . . . try a puff?

[**Master of Discipline** *drops to his knees, arms outstretched.
All eat and smoke*]

Master of Discipline [*singing*] 'Beloved berdu . . .' '. . . I
stand with you . . .' 'to lay the monster to rest' 'Dearly
beloveds . . . wubbub bee'

Quatro 7 Rosie [*amused, lowered voice*] . . . the Master's
fucking wasted . . .

Assistant . . . Instructor, I was meaning to say . . .

Instructor [*opening Kit Kat*] . . . Josh . . . call me Josh

Assistant . . . I'm so sorry . . . when he said . . . about
your sister . . . I should never have laughed . . . [*Nervous*

giggle] . . . shit . . .

Instructor It's OK.

Assistant I laugh when I'm nervous . . . I'm nervous all the time . . . at night, I sleep in my uniform in case someone finds out . . .

Instructor [*fond*] . . . I think you can stop that now

Assistant I'm such a coward . . .

Instructor That's not the word I'd use.

Assistant What is the word?

Instructor I'd go with brave.

Master of Discipline [*singing, still to the* Rainbow *tune*] '. . . the lady' . . . 'the lady sings' . . . 'the singer sees' . . . 'I anoint you' . . . [*Stops singing*] . . . With this dirty leak water. [**Master of Discipline** *dunks his head*]

Mono 16 Alex Are you hot, darling?

Mono 8 Rachel I could drink that bucket.

Quatro 6 Dawn Wait . . . but didn't he say they were on their way?

Assistant [**dialing*] . . . Base . . . base . . . do you read me...? [**Crackle and static*] Do you read me?

Quatro 22 Cat Sisters, I think one of the leaks may have sparked a fire somewhere

Master of Discipline [**singing, still to* Rainbow *tune*] 'Beloved berdu' . . . 'world without end' . . . [*Stops singing*] . . . forgot . . .

Quatro 7 Rosie Whose got the keys?

Instructor Vice took mine.

Assistant Assistants aren't allowed keys.

Instructor [*remembering*] The Master knows the code . . . What's the code, Master?

Master of Discipline [*singing*] . . . 'Wubbub Berdu' . . . 'Forgot you' . . . Forgot me' . . . 'Forgot to see' . . . [*Stops singing*] . . . Forgot!

Instructor Master?

Mono 15 Matty [*as all dunk in turn*] . . . There would have been an alarm

Mono 14 Anita If we need it, help will come.

Quatro 7 Rosie I wouldn't fucking bank on it.

Quatro 22 Cat Sisters, dunk those tops in the bucket.

Master of Discipline [*singing*] 'Purple and orange and blue' . . . 'six for blue' . . . [*Stops singing*] . . . hot . . .

Automated tannoy sound effect Fire . . . fire.

Quatro 9 Paula Put on a wet top, sisters

Mono 15 Matty Which one's mine?

Mono 14 Anita Any top, black or white

Master of Discipline [*as girls continue dunking and putting on tops, singing*] . . . 'set you free' . . . 'help us see' . . . 'six for blue?'

Mono 16 Alex Six, darling! Try six! Anything starting with six

[*****Instructor** *frantically punches in entry codes*]

Master of Discipline [*singing, always the same* Rainbow *tune*] . . . 'Berdu bee' 'music see' . . . 'six for blue' . . . [*Stops singing*] . . . forgot

Quatro 8 Beth It's not working!

[**Explosion*]

Instructor . . . The gas . . .

Master of Discipline [*singing*] . . . 'Set you free' . . . 'me see'...'see feel free' . . . 'Help me see' ... [*Stops singing*] . . . now!

[**Instructor** *turns on the music* – Lean on Me *by Bill Withers* – *can be heard*]

Quatro 9 Paula How do we all feel?

Automated tannoy sound effect FIRE . . . FIRE . . .

Mono 15 Matty We are all terrified?

Mono 14 Anita We are all angry?

Quatro 8 Beth We are all nervous?

Instructor We are all guilty?

Assistant We are all imposters?

Mono 16 Alex We were all cheated

Quatro 7 Rosie We are all islanders

Quatro 9 Paula We are all seers

Quatro 22 Cat We are all sisters

Quatro 6 Dawn We are all children

Mono 8 Rachel We are all dying

Mono 2 Ray We are all trapped

[**Fire alarm goes off*]

Quatro 9 Paula What can we see? [*Clapping*] . . . Now!

Instructor [*clapping*] . . . Sister

Mono 16 Alex [*clapping*] . . . Brother

Mono 8 Rachel [*clapping*] . . . Boyfriend

Mono 2 Ray [*clapping*] . . . Girlfriend

Quatro 6 Dawn [*clapping*] . . . Son

Mono 15 Matty [*clapping*] . . . Daughter

Mono 14 Anita [*clapping*] . . . Land

Quatro 7 Rosie [*clapping*] . . . Soil

Quatro 22 Cat [*clapping*] . . . Earth

Quatro 8 Beth [*clapping*] . . . Berdu!

[**Fire alarm*]

[**rattling at nearby bars. *The smashed camera gives off strobe flashes*]

Quatro 9 Paula Louder!

Mono 22 Cat Berdu!

Instructor Love!

Assistant Justice!

Quatro 9 Paula See it!

Mono 16 Alex Together!

All JUSTICE!

[**Sound of rewinding over fire alarm*]

[**Every sound and all music fades into a bell tolling over the lighting of suspended time*]

[*The fourth wall dissolves as everyone makes eye contact with the audience*]

Master of Discipline . . . My name is Alexander. I see colours, forwards and back. In my lifetime, the words dandelion, acorn, fern and kingfisher have disappeared from the *Oxford Children's Dictionary*. The history of coastal villages has slipped into the sea.

Mono 2 Ray Off shore detention camps have multiplied

Mono 16 Alex Those who care for the land are shot

Quatro 6 Dawn Farmers who home produce are sued

Quatro 22 Cat Fossil fuel companies bankroll dictators

Quatro 9 Paula Our earth and data are drilled and mined

Mono 8 Rachel Corporations contract out manslaughter

Quatro 8 Beth Unsafe buildings collapse and burn

Instructor I remember how courts were supposed to work

Assistant I remember that no one escapes unjudged

Quatro 22 Cat I remember that we can't drink oil

Mono 15 Matty I remember that money is not what we should love

Mono 14 Anita I remember when language deepened feeling

Quatro 7 Rosie I remember what freedom once meant

Master of Discipline I remember that when they say stay, we should go.

[*A crack of thunder]

[*The bell stops*]

[*Naturalistic lighting resumes*]

Security [*offstage*] . . . Stay put! Don't move! For your own safety, stay put!

Master of Discipline [*punching entry code in*] . . . Six ! [*Punched in*] . . . Three! . . . [*Punched in*] . . . One! . . . [*Punched in*] . . . Eight!

*Gate opens

[*The sound of fire and smoke*]

[*In sopping tops, all are poised to exit*

Quatro 9 Paula Sisters, brothers… . . .are we ready?

All Ready!

[*Lights flick off

[*Silence*]

[*The sound of the sea can be heard, then music – Stand By Me by Ben E. King – fourteen seconds in*]

Bluebeard's Wives

Bluebeard's Wives

by Helena Thompson

Duration

Seventy minutes

Bluebeard's Wives premiered at London's Institute of Contemporary Arts on 10th and 11th June 2003. It was presented by S.P.I.D. Theatre Company and was directed by Rachel Grunwald with design by Odelia Lavie and lighting by Tony Williams. Film for the production was by Daniel Wilson, with music by Marc Shearer and costume by Lucille Acevado-Jones.

The cast was as follows:

Sarah	Faith Hagerty
Bluebeard	Shaun Aston
Girls One, **Two** and **Three**	Faith Hagerty

Set

A room in a castle. The castle is an old-fashioned building with stone walls. It bears the signs of those who have lived there over the years. Although its occupants have overcome the bleak formality of its architecture, it does not feel like a family home. It is quite a daunting place.

Apart from mantelpiece, old paintings etc, the room specifically contains three doors leading to other parts of the castle, of which only one is open. The room also contains a large old chair in keeping with the antique décor of the place.

Characters

Sarah   Feisty working-class girl. Witty, loving, but very lonely. Given to talking to herself.

Bluebeard   A wealthy aristocrat. Austere, well-spoken and quick to judge. Capable of great tenderness. Bluebeard's presence on stage is initially that of a voice.

Girls One, Two and Three   Greedy, vineal and vain respectively. Dead females who are unaware of their immortality. They could be represented by film or live performance. **Sarah** and **Girls One**, **Two** and **Three** may double.

Act One

Enter rushing in through one of the doors
Sarah,

a pretty young girl, modestly dressed in well-made but rather dull attire in keeping with her old-fashioned surroundings

[**Sarah** *is carrying two sumptuous ball gown dresses scrunched up in her arms. The ball gowns are identical except for their colour. She wears an antique wedding ring which looks very large on her small young hand. She goes to the next door and opens it to reveal a third dress identical to the others except for the colour. Balancing the two dresses in her arms,* **Sarah** *struggles to pick up the third. As she does so, the door slams shut. Trying and failing to re-open it, she nearly drops her burden of three dresses and just manages to get them to the chair, onto which she collapses*]

Sarah [*feeling the arms of the chair*] Our Pete would love this. Wouldn't our Pete love this? Too small for 'im and too big for me, that's most chairs for y'.

[*Holding up the dress she just found*]

Sarah They're all me perfect fit! I never used to like dressing up. It was our Pete got me into it. He said to me, he said, 'Sarah! Sarah, even poor people don't wear dresses like Cinderella any more. Every body dresses up instead. Oh Sis you put on something nice now.' Brothers. They think they know it all don't they? Our Pete was goin' through a protective phase at the time. Y'know him, an' Mam. Because it was all nice dresses and not selling yourself short. Y'know Pete stopped drinkin' with the lads an' Mam stopped popping out for tea and the pair o' them started parading me about town instead. Y'know, where the ladies go!

[**Sarah** *begins to lay out the dress*]

Sarah Mind you I do miss 'em now, the pair o' them. Our
Pete was always into family pride. I said to him, I said,
'Pete, if you're gonna get all high an' mighty, couldn't
you've picked somethin' y'knew about? We're not exactly
the crème de la crème, are we?' 'Oh sis,' he said to me,
'y'never make the effort.' 'cause our Pete had given up on
me. So'd Mam. They thought I'd never get a sweetheart;
now they're all – settle down and make that husband of
yours proud. What're they like? So serious! 'A girl like
you's lucky to have a rich man lookin' after her.' They're
obsessed. Mind you, I'm pleased Mam seems happy for
me. Oh God. He must be home soon. What am I doin'
rushin' here with me arms full to bursting and he'll
be back to check up on me. Me famous husband, the
rumoured wife murderer. An' what's 'e like? Well, he
likes me to wear me hair short. Like a monk. He likes me
to be good. Like he likes to know where I am even if he's
somewhere else in the castle. If he doesn't know where
I am the minute he wants me, there's trouble. I've given
up arguin'. I said to him once, when his beard was blue
with rage, I said, 'Listen Bluebeard, if you can't always
find me right off the bat it doesn't mean I'm bein' bad,
y'know, or that I'm cheatin' on you. All it means, y'know,
is that I've found something to do with meself for a little
bit of the whole huge day.' Well did it do any good? I
could've been talkin' to meself. Couldn't I, I could've
been talkin' like this. [*Pause*] Even now I keep thinkin'
he's somewhere about the place, and he went off . . .
ages ago. They say, don't they, they say that once you've
lived with a man for a bit y'know them inside out. Well
I must've picked one with only an outside; I don't know
him at all. I'm not sayin' he's mysterious, me husband.
He's bleedin' predictable! He never talks. Mind you, I
think most of them are the same, aren't they? No good
with words, that doesn't make 'em freaks, does it? There's
not many's good with words. And men are lovely at first.
Y'know when they're wooin' you, before they've run out

of things to do, they're lovely then, all full o' promise an'
mystery an' some secret sort o' sufferin' that makes you
want to care for 'em however old they are. They'll chat
to your brother, they'll smile at your Mam, nothing is
too much trouble. But the minute, the very minute after
you've said yes – it stops being fun. It's like those music
boxes, isn't it? Oh it's lovely, isn't it – y'know, a magical
music box. That was the present he brought for me the
first time he came knocking at Mam's door. I was starin'
at the little thing pirhouetting around and around to
the music. His eyes were glued on me like that first time
when I played the piano as he sipped his champagne.
Me head was spinnin' again an' I was wonderin' who at
the hotel'd told him where I lived an' if he knew that
what I did was piano playin' of an evenin' an' that I was
as poor as he was rich. And I believed it was all magic.
An' that the person was alive an' the promise was real.
But it's mechanics, not magic, and whatever the secret
is it's not the sort that I can solve. If you try to stop the
spinning it just goes right on. If you beg for a bit of a
change once in a while or try to ask what it was up
to before you came along, 'Oh no. Right here is just
marvellous. Why go anywhere else? Why do anything
different?' When y'think about it, whoever made those
music boxes probably designed this castle.

[*Pause*]

Sarah I do like it here. I'm not unhappy. Not like Mother.
Mother's unlucky. Well, she says she is, y'know, she misses
father an' talks to him every day. Even though 'e's dead.
Well mother is unhappy. She loved her husband y'know. I
never knew him, it was before I was born. Apparently she
brought him tea one morning and found it stone cold
an hour later. Stone cold, cross me 'eart. Well apparently,
that's when she knew 'e wasn't goin' anywhere. An' I've
noticed, she's always dead worried if one of us leaves any
of their cuppa undrunk.

[*Pause*]

Sarah She told me not to marry Him. Jeez, when did she tell me? You know what she came out an' asked me? 'Do you love 'im?'

[*Laughs*]

Sarah Hey, imagine givin' this up! Imagine givin' this up in the name of . . . romance. Jeez, I've never been surer I wanted to marry someone in me life.

[**Sarah** *tries opening the door again*]

Sarah Bloody locked. Bloody locked me out. A right mess and nowhere to put it. Well it's not my fault.

[*She tries opening one of the other doors*]

Sarah Y'can't hide dresses under a chair, can y'? Every door in this bleedin' door trap opens right enough first off. Some castle. Slap bang in the middle of nowhere and miles from anywhere. Well the way I see it, I had to go explorin' – nothin' else to do. See what Mam would say is, a man's entitled to be rich and that's fine. If he likes his castle just so that's up to him. But it shouldn't stop me getting to know the place. If it makes me feel more comfortable. An' I know Mam's right. Marriage isn't that different from living at home, is it? There's no escape. You make the best of it, try and leave if there's a chance. But most of the time you just try to hide what you're aching for, when you're still busy searchin' y'self.

[*She empties out chocolates and underwear, make-up and perfume, from the dresses that are still scrunched up*]

Sarah Chocolates. Very rich. Make-up to make up after a lovers' spat. Perfume fit to knock a man's socks off. I shouldn't've taken all those dresses. Well, I tried to, like, tried to put 'em back.

[*She tries eating the chocolate and smelling the perfume and laying out the underwear and make-up*]

Sarah But y'know what This Place is like. If you find a game y'like playing it's bound to cheat on y'. Hey, it'd be brilliant though, wouldn't it? I just give 'im a kiss as 'e's pullin' me close and say, 'Oh look, sweetheart – I'm in this lovely ball gown and I'm just swayin' a little like this. Yeah. I've been good while you were away and now I fancy a little dance. You'll remember the steps, just close y'eyes. Just let y'self go an' tell me all about where you've been and who you were before I met y'. You'll hardly notice we're dancing. You'll hardly hear y'self.' And he'll give me that look, the one that looked lovely 'til I realised it wasn't desire at all; 'any tale too often told grows tiresome.' Y'know if I said to him . . . if I said I wanted to dance, he'd think I was tryin' to seduce 'im. Wouldn't 'e? Well . . . me, all packed up and dressed up, 'e'd think I was after 'is stuff. Well it's obvious isn't it? I'm not even particularly fond of 'is stuff – all this stuff, am I? I'm not. I think stuff is deadening. You try so hard to get it that when you do you're too tired. 'course it would all 've been different if I'd been born with a dream, like me Mam. 'cos they're different, aren't they? They live off it, y'see, the dream. The dreamers I call them. And good luck to them, I don't begrudge 'em anything. But I've never been in love like that. When I was little I thought a husband would make the stars tremble and the earth move. The only thing that trembled for me were me teeth in the cold of this place, what with Him lying there on our wedding night with his arms folded like the bed was an old coffin. But y'see, I'm not a dreamer am I? I mean, obviously, true love is always possible, like miracles, an' windfalls. It's possible but it's not really possible unless you've felt it, is it? Maybe I should've married a frog prince – y'know, one of those things that metamorphoses when y'kiss 'em. I was about, about six when I first heard the fairy tales. They were dead lovely. Life was a bit of a disappointment after that. I blame Perrault. Y'know, Charles. Y'see, what happened was, Perrault dug up the nasty old stories and um romanticised 'em. An' um the main thing he changed um was the ending. An' the other change, it was hardly a change at all, more of an assumption, was

that love exists, and love conquers all. Now y'see that's
what Perrault had said. An' loads of people believed 'im
– mainly girls I think. An' the littleuns. Well, y'would,
wouldn't y'. I mean, Charles Perrault, who's gonna call
'im a liar? I mean, say you're just having a heart to heart
with y'friend, an' y'friend introduces Charles Perrault
an' he's like her idol, an' he says to you, 'you must
wait for love,' well you'd wait patiently wouldn't y'? But
I tell you what you'll be waitin' – a bloody long time.
'cos Perrault, you see, 'e wasn't about the truth. No one
can predict the future. Love's just a nice idea people
like to believe in. But everyone remembers Perrault an'
he's still promisin' the impossible y'know an' that's why
Mam thought his tales made such great bedtime stories.
It's brilliant isn't it – gettin' people to believe in what
might not exist. It's like tellin' people about This Place
– most people sit at home imaginin' a fairy castle while
fools like me get lumbered with three hundred squillion
empty rooms. Well, when I first read the fairy stories I
thought they were true. I still think they could be true
actually. A real happy ending. That sounds good, doesn't
it? Really happy, 'Oh it all ended really happily, didn't
y'know.' 'Oh that sounds like a good story.' 'No it's not a
story . . .' A real happy ending.

[*She thinks about it*]

Sarah Oh shut up, I believed in happy endings.

[*Pause*]

Sarah Wait 'til 'e finds this mess. Well 'e said to be good,
didn't 'e? An' I don't know if I 'ave been. It's 'is religion,
isn't it? God pronounced it. 'Thou shalt not dress like a
harlet or create a mess for if thou dost, Bluebeard will
think you're 'avin' it off with someone else. 'What will
'e be like? What will 'e be like when 'e sees these dresses
on the floor? An' I wouldn't mind, only it's not even me
bloody fault about the dresses. Well, I just found 'em,
see. Whilst I was explorin' the castle. They felt so nice
y'see. But This Place is strange – it's big, y'know, so big

it has a brain of its own – 'The Shut Mind' I call it. Well, it's got these odd doors that open easy enough then shut and stay closed. Well, that's weird isn't it? I mean if a house has doors they're meant to open aren't they? Otherwise they'd be walls. But these are doors.

[*She looks to check that the single open door remains so*].

Sarah 'course after he's seen this mess, I don't think he'll quite see it that way. 'You've betrayed me! Stolen my wealth! Is this how you repay me? You wicked, wicked wife!'

[*She adopts a grand voice whilst making grand attempts to open the second door*]

Sarah 'Yes Bluebeard I do believe it is. I don't give a toss about you or your money 'cause I am bored out of my measely mind. Bluebeard! A man like you has no clue what a woman wants. Now count your coins whilst I find a man who knows how to have a laugh.'

[*She drops it*]

Sarah Hey, remember when Bluebeard started callin' for me? Oh God. Mother despaired of me and 'im. Her friends had told her Bluebeard was strange. I agreed with them. But Mother, she was fascinated by him. She would look at him for a long time. She said to me, she said, 'it may not be His fault – somethin' may have happened to 'im – but it appears that he's unnatural.'

[*She tries to open the third door*]

Sarah What Mam said the day I showed 'er the ring, it bounces 'round me head, 'you are a silly, silly girl.' Maybe I am. 'You've married a murderer, a lady killer.' Perhaps I 'ave.

[*Pause*]

Sarah It's no wonder, really, we're such an awful couple; must be a mother's curse. An' there was me when I was little, the only thing I ever wanted to do was please her.

I always wanted to make her proud. Be a real lady. But it was only the girls with rich parents who got to do that. The quiet ones. When Pete introduced me to one of his friends, the bloke said, 'she talks too much that one,' on account of how words was the only thing I've ever been in love with, an' it's just as well she's such a talker so as I don't have to talk to her.

I was never that interested in me brothers' mates after that. I became a recluse. I read so many books you would've thought I was a teacher. I was brilliant. Instead o' runnin' around to think, I became pensive, like that [*she twiddles her hair pensively*] an' I just seeped learnedness out of every pore. I was engrossed. 'I'm not comin' to town with y'.' 'I'm stayin' in again,' 'I'm not doin' this,' 'I'm not doin' that.' I'm half way through me book,' 'I'm on the last page,' 'I'm not coming,' 'I'd rather read.' But I never really had any books to read y'know. 'cept good old Perrault over an' over. After Pete's mate said that I used to say no whenever our Pete asked me to come out with 'im an' I really wanted to be dressin' up an' doin' whatever 'e was doin'.

[*She changes out of her dress*]

Sarah Can't y'be silly when you're little? I was dressin' up when Mam came round not so long ago. Wasn't I? I hadn't spoken to me family since the weddin'. I'm down some corridor, half way into an evening dress – not a ball gown, but the kind he likes me to wear. Anyway, what's the first thing that always happens when you're down a corridor half way into an evening dress? Right. There's a knock at the door. An' it's funny the way things seem to know when you're up to somethin', but they do; once you're down a corridor, puttin' on something that makes you look about six – it always follows that someone you never thought would visit should come along.

[*She changes into one of the ball dresses*]

Sarah Well I'm standin' there, like a tot, me skirt's around me ankles an' me slip's around me 'ead, so I thought I might as well go see who it was. 'course the door bleedin' bursts open before I got there. 'Sarah?' says Mam, 'Sarah, is that you?' I just sat there, nursin' me bruise an' lookin' a right state. 'It's you,' she said, 'it's me Sarah, I've come to see you an' y'husband' an' the way she said 'husband' sounded so gentle, an' the next thing, she's apologisin' for knockin' me over an' she's helpin' me to me feet an' carryin' me like a little kid an' settin' me down on a big sofa.

[*She puts on the make-up, completing the transformation from pretty girl to beautiful woman*]

Sarah Mam gave me a plant, all pretty in a pot, an' it didn't matter if it was a wedding gift or a house warming because all the flowers were budding away and the future smelled lovely. I'm sittin' there, me dress not properly on an' I'm thinkin' 'Well Mam, you always said Bluebeard'd make me sad, you've got me proper now, haven't y'? Well go on, spare me the misery, just have a dig an' let's get it over with; come on tell me all about your other child's family and littluns.' But she just sat there, starin', y'know really starin'. She didn't act high an' mighty at all. An' d'you know what she told me? When we were little . . .she wished she could've had some of my imagination. The two of us, sittin' there on this plush sofa, one all impressed and well behaved, the other a jibberin' wreck an' we're havin' a great time confessin' that when I was little we secretly admired each other. It made me sad. Like the two of us could've been mates – instead of mother an' daughter. We didn't half get on well together, that afternoon, on the sofa. We were rememberin' all sorts. I could've sat there forever – an' although she'd never've said it, I don't think Mam wanted it to end either. But then Bluebeard came in to take me to dinner. An' y'know somethin' – I didn't want to go. A feast we were eatin' in some candlelit setting, an' I didn't want it. But as Mam was leavin' . . . d'you know what she did? She hugged me – a big bear hug wi'

both arms – an' that hug had proper warmth. It was the
best hug I've ever had. Just before she said goodbye, she
said, 'You've done well Sarah', she said, 'I just want you
to know that our Pete's really proud of you, and so am
I.' An' then she, she took me hands and she said, 'Enjoy
y'self. Enjoy y'self with that husband who loves y'.'

[*Pause*]

Sarah As I was goin' to dinner, with Bluebeard's arm in
mine, I felt so alone. I don't know why. I'm sitting down
at the table with this glum look on me. An' in me 'ead
there's the voice that keeps sayin', 'he used to love me,
he used to love me.'

[**Sarah** *starts to cry*]

Sarah What happened? How did you end up here? This
man doesn't want y'. Do you remember how you thought
he'd be? Do you remember how he was before? He was
the sweetheart who wanted to marry y' an' when you said
yes y' made his day. An' even though he brought y' here,
to this cold place, you were both hopeful. For a while.
You still . . . looked forward. He used to . . . care. A lot.
Didn't he? He used to talk to y' – when the pair o' y' sat
together. Remember? Remember when they sang those
songs by the piano an' the silly buggers thought they
sounded smashin'. Stood by the fire, the pair o' them,
chattin' away and waltzing round the hotel ballroom?
An' the two o' them, dancin' for the first time – together.
And he held her close . . . and put his arm around her
waist . . . an' she knew what was an' would be. What
happened? What happened to the pair of them – did
somethin' happen or was it just that nothin' happened?
It would be . . . easier to understand if somethin' had
happened, if I'd let one o' our Pete's stupid friends
have his wicked way and get it over with, if, if there was
somethin' to blame. But there's nothin'. He stopped
talkin', an' before y' know it she's home alone amusin'
herself an' tryin'to work out if it was worth all the trouble.
And somewhere between meeting 'im an' settlin' here

her sweetheart became Bluebeard an' I became 'is wife
and what I can't remember is the day or the week or
the month . . .when it happened. When it stopped bein'
excitin'. When me sweetheart disappeared, an' I was all
alone in this huge castle.

[**Sarah** *smiles unconvincingly*]

Sarah He says he's glad I'm 'is wife. But he isn't. It's just
somethin' he says 'cause he won't talk about the others.
It's terrible – 'marry me,' isn't it? It's supposed to mean
the world. You can be mad an' sad an' losing your mind
an' if you ask him where he's been or why he's starin'
straight through y' or if he's thinkin' about the ones
what came before he'll say, 'don't you worry about that,
we're married now.' 'You're My Wife.' They should lock
it up. Keep it safe. It's the answer to everything. An'
d'you know somethin'? I've always wondered . . . why . . .
it is that if somebody goes and marries you, it seems to
automatically give them the right . . . to tell you less . . .
than people they only like, or people they just work with,
or people they don't even want to work with. See, see, if I
wasn't Bluebeard's . . . wife. If I was just the cook or some
lawyer – 'e'd be straight with me. An' 'e doesn't share
a bed with either o' them – 'e shares a bed wi' me! An'
he never touches me when we're under the covers. He
never answers me questions. When he talks to me at all.
It's funny isn't it – 'Be My Wife'?

[*Pause*]

Sarah An' I know what you're sayin'. You're sayin' what
Mam always said – why don't you stand up for y'self'? An'
the fact of the matter is – I don't know how. I don't know
how anyone can change a situation in which a young
married woman has everythin' she ever wanted, an' no
one to share it with. I don't know how . . . I just know that
if you described it to me, a woman whose rich husband
wants her always to be a girl, I'd say y'were tellin' me a
joke. I don't know why 'e won't talk when 'e always used
to love me. I don't know why I feel so empty. An' I hate

meself for thinkin' so dirtily when I've never been dirty
before. I hate the joke of it. Because now that I'm ready
an' desperate an' yearning for something to fill me up,
I can't feel romantic anymore. I'm talkin' to meself to
drown out the silence an' I'm tryin' not to feel anything.
I've been talkin' an' feelin' this way for longer than I
can remember now. Even before I ended up right in the
middle of this terrible maze of a place, I was talkin' in me
'ead. An' I'm frightened. I'm terrified if y'want to know.
I'm terrified that if I danced, he wouldn't dance with me
an' I'd find it was impossible on me own – I couldn't any
more. I used to be able to. But when I stopped doin' it for
so long – I'd forgotten how. So I stay. Stay good. An' . . .
an' if I never laugh again – well . . . sod it. I mean, after
all, what's so great about smile lines? Smiling's only what
keeps y'young, isn't it? An' this place isn't young. 'Older
than time – a castle so fine – Sarah be mine.' Other
couples aren't like me an' Bluebeard are they?

[*Sarah laughs*]

Sarah An' anyway, a spot o' perfume an' I can pretend
I'm at the ball. Hey, look. [*puts on perfume*] Look at how
I move. Smell my scent. Can't you just feel the perfume,
the dress. Would y'look, look at that woman, that lovely
young woman – doesn't she look promisin', all dressed
up, wearin' her perfume, in a fairytale castle.

[**Sarah** *hugs herself and smiles, the walls of the room flash blue*]

Sarah What the bleedin' hell was that? Somethin' flashed.
Was it something I said? Oh I'm not talking anymore.
Did somethin' bloody flash or didn't it?

Sarah [*suddenly*] He'll be home soon.

[**Sarah** *stuffs the chocolate, perfume, make-up and slips under
the chair*]

Sarah Oh Jeez oh Jeez. Me dresses.

[**Sarah** *gathers up the dresses and stuffs them under the chair
too*]

Sarah Perfume, chocs, dresses, make-up, perfume, chocs, dresses, make-up. Oh God, oh God, please say he won't mind. Oh I feel sick. That chocolate is somethin' else – I do feel sick. Oh God, perfume, chocs, slips, dresses, make-up. I'm folding these dresses nicely.

[**Sarah** *puts the dresses under the chair*]

Sarah Well y'never know, Sarah – he could've left them for you; tonight, a new dress . . . tomorrow . . . a party.

[**Sarah** *clasps her hands in supplication. A key drops from the keyhole of the middle door. She approaches the door*]

Sarah Oh. I know I wasn't imaginin' it. I know I saw it flashin'.

[**Sarah** *takes the key. She hesitates. She goes to one of the locked doors*]

Sarah It's been like bein' Goldilocks with all these rooms an' every soddin' sound you think it's a big bear comin' for you – he's found out you've bin at the porridge.

[**Sarah** *opens the middle door to reveal an antique sword. She reaches out to touch the sword and places the key beside it. The door she entered through slams shut and she moves away*]

Sarah God I know . . . it's my fault, I know. I should never've annoyed 'im like that, not with 'im keepin' big swords about the place. But I don't mind it bein' my fault. Just, just do me a big favour God an' don't let him think I don't want him. Don't let anything've happened to 'im while he's away. An' don't let him be angry wi' me. Please.

[**Sarah** *clasps her hands in supplication. Another key drops from the other closed door, surprising her. She takes the key and opens the next locked door to reveal a large old wedding cake covered in cobwebs. She steps in to inspect the cake and the door with the sword slams shut. She rushes back into the room and puts the key in the lock*]

Sarah So long I've been creepin' around wonderin' what's
in This Place. An' now I find this. Keep thinkin' about
the women he married, keep thinkin' about the women
who wore these dresses . . . it was not bein' allowed to
wear this sort o' thing that started the argument, wasn't
it? I'd tried hard, hadn't I? Made meself look nice. An'
that takes a while when you've only dull clobber like
this. I mean, alright. So he says he likes me the way I
am, but . . .he stands in the hall, doesn't he, an' he looks
at me. Just stares. Doesn't say anything about the way I
look. He stands there with this puzzled look on, an' he's
starin' at me undone top button, studyin' it, y'know as
though it gives me away. Well I just ignored him, didn't
I? I just stood there, opposite. Well, eventually, he goes,
'What's this. What. Is. This?' I said to him, I said, 'Well,
when I put it on, it was an evening dress, and as neither
of us has a magic wand, I'm assuming it's still an evening
dress.' Well he starts pacin' the hall an' he says, 'I am
not . . .supporting a whore,' honest to God, an' he grabs
me neck. Well I'm gaspin' there, aren't I? Hardly able to
breathe. His hand's tight round me neck as he fumbles
to do up me top button an' he's screamin' to the
heavens of the castle; 'cos 'e does that when 'e's pissed
off, doesn't 'e. 'I am her husband in the eyes of God,'
he's tellin' the heavens, 'An' how does she dress?' Well
of course, the heavens never answer him so whenever
he asks a question he always answers it himself. He goes,
'Let it be known what she wears. An unbuttoned dress,
she wears an unbuttoned dress.'

[**Sarah** *clasps her hand in supplication and cranes her ear to
hear if a key drops. It doesn't; she turns to see this. She tries
clasping her hands again. Still no key. She turns and takes a step
towards the door she entered through, ripping a little of her dress.
The door she entered through drops a key, to her surprise. She goes
to take the key as she chatters blithely on*]

Sarah Well I don't know what possessed me but while he
was screamin' at the heavens, I pick meself up and hitch
up me skirt.

[*As* **Sarah** *opens the door she entered through to reveal a mirror, the other open door shuts and sucks the key back through the lock. She puts the key in her cleavage and hitches up her skirt*]

Sarah When the Big Fight was over he left a note.

[*She drops her skirt*]

Sarah I woke up the next day an' there it was. 'Do whatever you want, but don't degrade yourself.' 'Y'what?' I said, and turned over. 'This Place,' it said. 'This Place is yours as well as mine.' That surprised me a bit. 'You will find out what to do and how to do what you want. Do whatever you want, but don't degrade yourself.' Well that's when I started openin' the doors. I ended up . . .I was goin' mad . . . I ended up runnin' around the place. I heard the door slam, and he was gone. But I couldn't stop laughin' then. I couldn't stop laughin' because I knew I was gonna do it. I knew I was gonna explore every inch o' the place. An' everything was such fun, wasn't it? So today I ended up here, y'know the way you do when you've been running around 'til you get to the place where it all joins up?

[**Sarah** *clasps her hands in supplication once more, then repeats the gesture. She turns and takes a step towards the door that revealed the sword, ripping a little more of her dress. The door drops no key, to her surprise*]

Sarah Well as I was on me way here I looked at all me stuff an' y'know I started wonderin' at what I'd found. All the stuff in me arms. Well I hadn't really thought about it – just taken it with me – but I thought oh, look at this, it's just what you've been wanting. So I thought about how I'd found it, the chocolate, an' perfume, an' dresses, an' that's when I realised. Well what had I done but found his dead wives' stuff? His dead wives. I thought to myself, 'Calm down Sarah.' Because I always get in a tizz. Well those dresses felt so sexy it was like they said, 'I suppose you would think us exotic, seein' as your clothes are so dull.' Well I know I shouldn't've got jealous but that got me seethin' an' I heard meself sayin', 'Oh no, I don't like sexy clothes, not at all – and what's more Bluebeard loves me to look plain. Well, I must be on me way – I've still got some more pressies to find. Bluebeard leaves pressies for me when he goes away, I expect he thought you might entertain me. Off we go,' an' I'd snatched up those dresses like they'd been mine all along.

[**Sarah** *clasps her hands in supplication once more, then repeats the gesture. She turns and takes a step towards the door that revealed the sword, ripping a little more of her dress, and undoes the top button of her dress. A key drops. She goes to take it as she chatters blithely on*]

Sarah Well I've done me best to be dutiful. Here he is, rulin' the roost, goin' off when he pleases without even tellin' me where. 'You're my little cog,' he used to say, 'the most important part of the whole machine.' Well I would smile, and do as I was told, an' he would say, 'You're so good, aren't you? You do whatever you are told.' An' the thing is, I would nod. I'd hardly been there a week an' I was feelin' like some damsel who didn't know distress until she got rescued and lost her mind. Completely under his thumb, I was. Well it was when he disappeared after the Big Fight that me head cleared.

[**Sarah** *opens the door to reveal the sword once more and puts the key in another part of her cleavage. The other open door slams shut*]

Sarah Men – they can't half make y'feel crap, can they? I'd spent that long tryin' to look good an' he goes an' says somethin' like that.

[**Sarah** *clasps her hands in supplication once more, then repeats the gesture. She turns and takes a step towards the door that revealed the cake, ripping a little more of her dress, and undoes another button of her dress. A key drops. She goes to take it as she chatters blithely on*]

Sarah I'd even convinced meself that I was a bit of a princess, that those gossips had nothing on us. That we had a fresh start together, all clean. I'd got blurry eyed thinkin' about him an' me an' how we'd got another chance to see the loveliness in each other, the loveliness no one else could see, an' how it transfigures an' transforms an' how we weren't neither of us dirty now. Sittin' here on me own, havin' thrown the note away – I was suddenly the naughtiest, least deserving little wench in the country. Me dress was the tartiest I'd ever seen, an' instead of being Bluebeard's wife I was a poor harlot and nothing more. 'You're gonna tart y'self up?' yelled the voice in me head. 'I am,' I said. 'And what does Bluebeard have to say about that?'

[**Sarah** *opens the door to reveal the cake and the other open door slams shut. She keeps the key in her knickers*]

Sarah 'You whore.'

[**Sarah** *clasps her hands in supplication once more, then repeats the gesture. She turns and takes a step towards the door that revealed the mirror, ripping a little more of her dress. She tries to open it but the key to the mirror door no longer works*]

Sarah What is it to be cherished by a man? To be held and trusted and warmed by something that loves?

[**Sarah** *clasps her hands in supplication once more, then repeats the gesture. She turns and takes a step towards the door that revealed the mirror, ripping a little more of her dress, and undoes the top button of her dress. A key drops. She goes to take it as she chatters blithely on*]

Sarah I feel awful, hitching me skirt up like that. I mean, I don't know what he must've thought and I'm dead ashamed. But at the time all I was thinkin' was how me Mam was proud o' me. Completely proud. She believed that it was possible for me to be some marvellous, married, poor-girl-come-good. I wondered what I looked like an' tried to imagine the woman Mam thought she'd been talkin' to. In her eyes I was no longer Sarah the little sister, the girl who scared the boys, or Sarah the chatterbox. I had become the lovely, accomplished, wife of Bluebeard; I was Bluebeard's wife.

[**Sarah** *clasps her hand in supplication once more, then repeats the gesture. She turns and takes a step towards the door with the sword, ripping a little more of her dress. She undoes the top button of her dress, then another. A key drops from the door with the mirror. She goes to take it and goes immediately to open the door, which opens to reveal the sword. She keeps the key. As she chatters blithely on, she clasps her hands in supplication once more, then repeats the gesture, turns and takes a step towards the door with the cake, ripping a little more of her dress before trying and failing to open the door with the key to the cake door . . . by this point her repeated actions are coming to resemble a mechanical dance like that of a wind-up doll*]

Sarah An' even if I couldn't see meself that way, even if me stone cold husband had just called me a whore – the point is that our Pete sees a different me. Believed that I could be this wonderful woman. I'm pleased to've put on this dress. I don't think of it as His dead wife's, I just think it's beautiful. Ever since the moment I put it on, I've been dignified. An' I'm still dignified. I'm the lady o' the house.

[*Having undone a button of her dress, then another, and another, the door drops a key and* **Sarah** *opens it to reveal the cake once more. The keys about her person clatter to the ground and she repeats her actions in pursuit of the next key, chattering louder and louder as she 'dances'*]

Sarah An' I'm gonna open these doors and know me own castle and not be afraid or ashamed. What's there to care about! I can do anything now. I'll be invincible, I'll make dreams come true, just like the fairy stories, only real this time. I'll be Bluebeard's favourite wife.

[**Sarah** *clasps her hand in supplication once more, then repeats the action. She turns and takes a step towards the door with the mirror, dancing in her underwear. Having unbuttoned another button, then ripped her dress, and taken it off, the door fails to drop a key*]

Sarah Course, I'm terrified really. But I'm not gonna let it stop me. I don't mean I won't be careful – I've got that sword. And the cake – it's only a cake, it's only a cake. I like to dance an' if he asks me why I've done what I've done I shall say the castle made me do it.

[**Sarah** *clasps her hand in supplication once more, then repeats the action. She turns and takes a step towards the door through which she entered, dancing in her underwear. The door drops a key, which she doesn't notice. She rips her underwear and the door drops another key. She goes to take it and opens the final door, revealing a projected film or live performing* **Girl One**, *almost naked, dancing in her underwear just like her. As the girl dances* **Sarah** *dances too, enjoying the liberation of her movements*]

Girl One 'I went out of my mind, banged my chest, and ripped my clothes into shreds. Nothing; until, with a sigh I cried out, began to drift away, and the walls would give me a key.

Girls Two *and* **Three** *appear – as film or live – from the other doors*

[*The girls join in the dance; these girls – projected film or live – are likewise dressed erotically like Sarah and dancing slightly out of synch with each other. They share* **Sarah**'s *face and figure but each has different coloured hair in a different hair style. They repeat themselves as* **Girl One** *loops her speech.* **Sarah** *also speaks. Their simultaneous words are as follows*]

Girl Two Nobody but Bluebeard could wind me up. I didn't make this music, no, I simply opened the door; even before people like you arrive and I get the key. I've felt haunted ever since he loved me.

Girl Three I know; for he himself, he would often degrade me. He'd strip me down, make me dance, he'd nip me.

Sarah Look what I've found! Some friends to talk to! Some friends who look like me!

[*The* **Girls**' *speech reaches a crescendo*]

[**Girls One**, **Two** *and* **Three** *and* **Sarah** *dance as the girls continue to loop their speech. A voice is heard*]

Voice You have shown your degradation.

Sarah I'm dancin'! I'm dancin'!

Voice Put on your clothes.

Sarah Come and join us!

Voice Never. You have stripped yourself half naked.

Sarah That's right! And it's lovely! Lovely to feel the air on me skin. I don't look too bad, do I? Don't move too bad, either. Me pals look pretty good too, I reckon.

Voice They're whores! Like you!

Sarah Charming. If a woman can't undress at home, I don't know what This Place is coming to.

Voice You're not alone.

Sarah You think I ever listen to the voice in me 'ead!

Voice I'm your husband.

[**Sarah** *stops dancing*]

Voice [*quietly*] I wasn't always like this.

Sarah [*trying to compose herself*] I – [*Pause*] I –

Voice You?

Sarah Actually, if we're bein' honest now, y'were always like this. A great boomin' voice wi' no desire t'actually be with me.

Voice I was different before we met.

[**Sarah** *blocks her ears*]

Voice I was mortal then.

[**Sarah** *desperately hums a nursery rhyme tune to herself*]

Voice My life was shorter than eternity.

Sarah This isn't real. [*Pause*] This is me imagination. Me and me imagination, that's what Mam always said, like the best o' friends, / like

Voice This is the voice that proposed to you!

Sarah [*unblocking her ears*] Well where are y'then? [*Sing song*] Oh Bluebeard, y'can come out now. You've had y'little game. Where are y'Bluebeard?

Voice I'm here.

Sarah Y'where?

Voice Within these walls.

Sarah Y'what?

Voice Within what surrounds you.

Sarah [*pause*] You've been spyin' on me?

Voice You've cheapened yourself for the wealth behind my doors.

Sarah That's wealth, is it? An old cake, a crumby sword an' a mirror?

Voice Do not mock me!

Sarah [*laughing*] But y'so funny! Hiding away pretending you've turned to stone. Y'not even man enough t'show y'face!

Voice There are things here you will never understand.

Sarah I've explored this place an' y'right, it's a loony bin.

Voice You cheated me.

Sarah Any girl getting treated like part of the furniture would've done what I've done, if they didn't top themselves first.

Voice Some of us would like that luxury.

Sarah Wouldn't we just! Because Bluebeard, Mr Not
Here, Mr Great Flashin' Nobody, y'may as well be a
wall for all the care you've shown me. I'll call you me
husband because that's who you say you are but what I
really need is someone to talk to, someone who'll notice
how natural I look in this dress. I mean, I know I'm not
the first woman to wear it an' I probably won't be the
last. But I like the way I look, which is more than can be
said for some. I know that whatever happens I'm a lovely
young woman an' you, you're a thing, a great useless
thing without a flicker o' feelin' in y'.

[*The* **Girls** *continue to dance but their looped words decrescendo
down to a whisper*]

Sarah An' isn't it funny, but if you're with someone night
and day who doesn't talk, who's sort of eaten up with
bitterness and the proper problem of being stuck with
themselves who they hate – well y'like, start to think that's
how things are. You feel bitter too, you think it's bad to
be alive. An' you're not a girl or a woman or anyone any
more, you're just a thing. I tried to like, keep me eyes
closed. Because it was easier bein' Sleeping Beauty. I
kept tryin' to think of other things, but I couldn't. It was
just there in me 'ead. An' this thought was . . .all I am . . .
is married. And I don't want that. I mean, Mam'd be
disappointed, it's terrible to have a daughter who doesn't
obey the one man who'll provide for her. But I haven't
gone mad. I haven't. I'm not losin' it. I've no regrets.
I've had a good time exploring This Place because it's
never been me 'ome. Everythin' that happens here
happens because o' you, Bluebeard, an' who you were,
an' I know nothin' o' that and you know nothin' o' me.
Not a thing. I see you lookin' at me but I don't think
you're seeing properly. An' what I mean to say is that
you don't love me. An' what you've been sayin' is that
you do, pretending you've rescued me from drudgery
and glumness. An' all the time that you've been watchin'
me, an' when I thought you'd gone, an' in the long time
bein' on me own traipsing through This Place I didn't

know what it was I wanted to do, or who I was really. An' I've been frettin' for a feelin' an' wonderin' why all those women Mam feels sorry for are so much happier than me. Even though they're poor they're not as dead . . . as me. An' what's killin' me is the terrible suffocation o' pretendin' to be somethin' for a man who's completely compassionless in a place that's just his way of spyin' to make sure I do / what he wants.

[*Dust splutters from the walls.* **Sarah** *stops talking*]

Sarah Are y'makin' this happen? [*Silence*] It's like – it's like the walls are weeping. [*The voice of* **Bluebeard** *audibly weeps*] [**Sarah** *awkwardly touches the walls to see if she can make the dust stop falling*] Maybe I was overdoin' it a bit. Y'can't help getting' bored o' me can y'? I get bored o' me.

Bluebeard [*previously referred to as* **Voice**] I wasn't bored.

Sarah Just more interested in y'castle.

Bluebeard I wanted to hold you close always, to dance forever with your pretty soul.

Sarah Why didn't y'?

Bluebeard I was afraid.

[**Sarah** *stops dabbing at the walls in surprise*]

Bluebeard The way a girl can change is fearful. She keeps her sweet exterior but her heart just disappears. The sight of money sucks her soul, or the proof that she's desired. Her beauty becomes a trap, a game, for me a / living hell

Sarah And what d'y'call this?

Bluebeard [*quietly*] I did not chose to live like this.

Sarah Most men show their faces when they're talkin' to y'.

Bluebeard Most men have not turned to stone.

[*The walls stop their spluttering*]

Sarah [*gently*] How's about just turnin' y'self back?

[**Sarah** *thinks again, then gives the wall a quick and wary kiss before retreating*]

Bluebeard Stop!

Sarah If you're under some kind o' spell I just thought a kiss might help. Y'know . . . [**Sarah** *giggles nervously*] if you think a frog's a prince you just give it a kiss / and

Bluebeard I am not a frog!

Sarah No. [*Pause*] No. [*Pause*]. Bloody Perrault. Y'know, Charles, / he pretends

Bluebeard, Girl One, Two and Three A false kiss is the worst kind of betrayal!

[**Sarah** *is stunned. She turns to the dancing girls and registers for the first time how strange they are. They continue dancing as she speaks, and though their chanting gets louder they stop their chanting in order to speak to her*]

Sarah Why is he crying?

Girl One Why is he crying?

Girl Two You betrayed him

Girl Three You betrayed him.

Sarah No I haven't.

Girls No I haven't.

Sarah What / are

 Girls We're just like you.

Sarah [*trying to touch the girls*] You're . . . images.

Girl One Images

Girl Two Images

Girl Three Image is everything

 Girl One Everything

Girl Two Everything

Girl Three Image is / everything

Sarah No it's not. It's not flesh. It's not flowers. Or huggin' y'Mam. It's not readin' stories an' cryin' 'cause they're so sad. That's the stuff that makes you glow.

Girl Two [*during the following sequence* **Girls One**, **Two** *and* **Three** *look at each other as they speak*] Flowers?

Girl Three Mam?

Girl One Stories?

Girl Two Stories?

Girl Three Stories?

Girl Two You don't need them, except to die!

[**Girls One**, **Two** *and* **Three** *laugh and stop looking at each other*]

Girl Three Do you want to die?

Sarah I don't want to live forever.

Girl One You're in Bluebeard's castle.

Girl Two No one dies in Bluebeard's castle.

Sarah 'course they do. Only fairytales have ghosts.

Girl Three [*during the following sequence the* **Girls** *stop looking at each other*] Ghosts?

Girl Two Ghosts?

Girl One What are ghosts?

[*Pause*]

[**Sarah** *turns to* **Bluebeard** *as* **Girls One**, **Two** *and* **Three** *stop looking at each other*]

Sarah Mam was right, wasn't she? [*Pause*] What've you done to them?

Bluebeard I haven't done anything.

Sarah Don't lie, Bluebeard. Tell me what I deserve to know.

Girls One, Two and Three Know.

Bluebeard No!

Sarah Monster!

Girls One, Two and Three Monster!

Sarah You killed these women.

Girl One Killed

Girl Two Killed

Girl Three Killed

Sarah [*she bangs her fists against* **Bluebeard** *the walls*] D'you think I'm blind? I can see a dead person blinkin' me in the bloody eye. You killed them for being human, didn't you, for hankering after a bit of air in a place too dead to breath – for wantin' some excitement, heaven forbid, in this hellish coffin you're so keen on. What did they do? Eat a bit of y'cake? Look in y'mirror? Open y'doors? That's not degradation! That's being alive!

[**Sarah** *hits the walls harder until she exhausts herself*] I'm alive! Why don't you murder me? Murder me!

Girl One Murder me!

Girl Two Murder me!

Girl Three Murder me!

Sarah Murder me like you murdered your wives!

[**Sarah** *tires of hitting the walls*]

Bluebeard Don't stop

[*Pause*]

Sarah Pervert.

Bluebeard [*quietly*] I almost felt something.

[**Sarah** *regards the walls oddly*]

Bluebeard May I not crave the touch of my wife, though she cheats and deceives and degrades me still? I've longed for you since before we met. I dream of your hair even now that it's gone. I've lain awake with wanting you, telling myself that my restraint could keep you pure.

[**Sarah** *moves towards the nearest open door but stops at the sound of* **Bluebeard**'s *voice*]

Bluebeard You foolish, foolish child. Don't you know where you are?

[*The doors slam shut*]

Sarah Pete'll come for me. Y'can't keep me brother out.

Bluebeard No one leaves Bluebeard's castle.

Sarah You left for our wedding.

Bluebeard *and* **Girls One, Two** *and* **Three** We came back.

[**Sarah** *turns to see* **Girls One**, **Two** *and* **Three** *speaking*]

Girl One [*from the door with the cake*] I was Bluebeard's wife. Once upon a time, I was bored like you. I had everything I wanted, and when I found more, more than I had imagined, I tried to steal it all. When he found me out and beckoned me [**Girl One** *beckons as part of her dance*] he wasn't like this, he was beautiful, the way he spoke . . . and when I went to him he gave me everything. He left me, and I was sorry. I sniffed my body for his smell, I dreamed his touch and lay in the places we had been together. There was nothing to do.

[**Sarah** *nibbles absentmindedly on the chocolate beneath the chair*]

Girl One I ate everything, I drank everything, and grew fat, so fat I died.

[**Girl One** *holds out a cake like the one behind the door.* **Sarah** *stops eating the chocolate in disgust*]

Girl Two I was Bluebeard's wife. Once upon a time, I was bored like you. I had everything I wanted though my mind would wander; I stumbled on Bluebeard's trust. He tried to hide it from me and I could not help but wonder why. I hid my own unfaithful thoughts. Who he was was a secret, yet his faith in me surprised. I told my lover to come with me and live upon my husband's wealth, but the breath on my neck soon told me we were discovered. When my husband beckoned me [*she beckons as part of her dance as* **Sarah** *caresses herself*] he wasn't like this, he was a hard-faced, stilted man. He screwed me the way I like to be screwed, stripped me of everything and gave me a sword; how I loved that sword. I loved it better when my lover left me for a girl as rich as I had been [*she holds out a sword like the one behind the door, in sudden fear* **Sarah** *holds her arms rigid at her side*] That sword was smooth and dangerous, hard and long. [**Girl Two** *'discovers' the sword behind the door as part of her dance*] I slit myself.

Girl Three I was Bluebeard's wife. Once upon a time, I was bored like you. I had everything I wanted, and I grew dissatisfied. [**Sarah** *covers her eyes in fear*] He kept me always in his sight, and when he found me painting my face, he beckoned me away [*she beckons as part of her dance*]; didn't you, my husband . . . I went and saw what a fool I was. I saw the pictures of his wives and hated them for having had him first. He hadn't told me of them and to spite him I called him a wife murderer. I spread the rumours round the town and said I didn't want him. His beard turned blue and I called him hideous. I heard him crying as he touched himself and I tried to block my ears. Staring in the mirror, I disliked what I saw. My body changed and wasted away. [**Sarah** *covers her eyes as* **Girl Three** *peers into a mirror*] I faded.

Sarah [*approaching* **Girl One** *and shouting angrily*] It's your fault.

Girl One [*slowly repeating her speech as* **Sarah** *talks to her*] I was Bluebeard's wife. Once upon a time, I was bored / like you.

Sarah I don't care if y'were bored!

Girl One I grew fat/ so fat I died.

Sarah You're disgustin'!

Girl Two [*slowly repeating her speech as* **Sarah** *turns to her*] I was bored like you. / I had everything

Sarah I'm not like you.

Girl Two I told my lover to / come with me

Sarah I haven't got a lover.

Girl Two He screwed me the way I like to be screwed.

Sarah I don't like to be screwed.

Girl Two How I loved that sword.

Sarah [*addressing the walls as* **Girl Two** *continues to speak and dance*] What's screwing?

Girl Two Smooth and dangerous, hard and long.

Sarah Is this what y'think o' me?

Girl Three [*repeating her speech slowly as* **Sarah** *continues*] I was Bluebeard's wife. / Once upon a time, I was bored like you.

Sarah [*impersonating* **Bluebeard***'s voice*] 'Your little cog?' 'Here's a white dress little cog?' 'Don't kiss me little cog?'

[**Sarah** *throws her white dress at* **Girl Three**]

Girl Three I went and saw /what a fool I was.

Sarah Make 'em stop!

Girls One, **Two** and **Three** I was Bluebeard's wife. I was Bluebeard's wife. / I was Bluebeard's wife.

Sarah MAKE 'EM STOP! [**Girls One**, **Two** *and* **Three**'s *voices fade away*]

Sarah [*trying to cover her near nakedness*] I'm sorry. [*Pause*] I'm sorry, I'm sorry.

[*Coins pelt from the walls*]

Bluebeard What are you sorry for? [*Pause*] Your loved one pretending to love you? And your next love? And the next, and the next? The same pain over and over, everything the same until you couldn't hurt or tell the difference and all you felt was feeling less like time had just . . . stopped? Little girl, living death is something else.

[*The pelting stops.* **Sarah** *picks up the coins. She stacks them in a pile beside the wall*]

Bluebeard Take them.

Sarah I don't want them.

Bluebeard Then why did you marry me?

[**Sarah** *is silent*]

Sarah I liked you. I still like you.

Bluebeard You married me because you liked me? [**Bluebeard** *laughs*]

Sarah I've done nothing as terrible as them.

Bluebeard What've they done?

Sarah They . . . used you. Over and over.

Bluebeard How?

Sarah By saying they wanted y'.

Bluebeard You said you wanted me.

Sarah All they wanted was nice food, nice clothes, some other young man.

Bluebeard And what do you want?

[*In the silence* **Sarah** *hugs herself*]

Bluebeard I was a man once. With a man's feelings and a man's sense of loss.

[**Sarah** *leans against the walls*]

Sarah [*pause*] If I had known, I would never have laughed at you.

Bluebeard [*laughing again*] Why shouldn't you laugh? I've had cause for suspicion and it has drained my feelings. I am bricks and mortar, nothing more.

Sarah No.

Bluebeard First my heart froze, then my beard turned blue.

Sarah This isn't you.

Bluebeard I didn't trust you before, and now I trust you less.

Sarah I never meant to betray you. [*Pause*] You saw me dancing, yeah. At first I wanted the keys, y'right there, but I also wanted to know the truth. And now I do. I admit, I lost control – but when I opened that door, I saw meself. I saw meself properly.

Bluebeard You admit that you are like my other wives.

Sarah Don't make fun of me.

Bluebeard It's you who mock! You've mocked me and betrayed me ever since we met, and you mock me the more by pretending you are otherwise.

Sarah That's not true.

Bluebeard Look at yourself. You're worse than them.

Sarah I'm not that bad.

Bluebeard They admitted what they wanted me for. You, even now I've found you out, continue to lie.

[*The walls flash blue for the second time*]

[**Bluebeard** *laughs for the third time*]

Sarah [*against her will she finds herself repeating her dance*] I'm tired, Bluebeard, I'm too tired for this. I know you're not to blame, I know it's me too, but I can't keep goin' through the motions. Because if you've imagined how somethin' is gonna be, sort of kept it glowin' inside your head, it wears you out when it's not the picture. I mean from the moment you proposed I had this image o' us livin' here, an' sharing a life; but when it got to it, it wasn't a bit like that. Because when it got to it I didn't feel at all lovely like a newlywed. I felt pretty depressed actually.

[*In the course of the dance she tries and fails to grab her white dress*]

Sarah A bit stupid too an' awfully, awfully young. I didn't feel wanted. Like, like if I'd ever tried to talk to y'about what your wives were like, well you'd go, 'it doesn't matter.' An' you'd shut up. An' it was the worst thing because I'd thought we'd grow an' blossom from what we'd been and you . . .well you'd said you wanted me and now I didn't know what to think. What I kept thinkin' about was how you'd lived so long before me, with all those other women. An' one way or another I could never match up. I thought to meself, I've sold meself really – sold my life to you, because . . .all you'd given me was money. I'd allowed meself to be bought when what I really wanted was to be loved. To be loved beyond me own imaginin'.

[*Unwillingly she approaches the wall in the part of the dance where she goes to take the key*]

Sarah You . . . y'shouldn't've . . . taken me away if you weren't goin' to share y'life. Not if y'weren't gonna ever mention y'past. Why . . . why did y' . . . promise me so much an' never so much as properly touch me?

[*She throws herself against the walls and kisses them. Her will is restored to her*]

Sarah I wanted to be touched.

[*The walls flash for the third time, and retain their glow. During the sonnet* **Sarah** *dresses herself while* **Bluebeard***'s voice melts into a more human sound speaking with the girls, who dance slower as if in slow motion to suggest the halting of time.* **Bluebeard***'s humanised voice is capitalised while the other three styles indicate which of* **Girls One**, **Two** *and* **Three** *are speaking*]

No body but YOU CAN SEEM SIMPLY *I*
went out of my mind, banged my chest WAYWARD,
and ripped my clothes into shreds. Nothing; Blue
beard *until,* SARAH, **I** *with a sigh,*
I cried out, BUT IT IS ME YOU SERVE; could
wind me up. I didn't make this **know; for**
he himself, music, no, I simply DO
opened the door; **he would** even before
WHAT YOU WANT, **often degrade me**. **He'd strip**
me down, *began to drift away,* **make me**
dance, BUT JUST DON'T DEGRADE YOURSELF. *And the*
walls people like you arrive **he'd nip**
me *gave me a key.* and I get the key.
I've felt haunted ever since he loved me.

[**Girls One**, **Two** *and* **Three***'s dancing becomes gentler, slower and weaker as the blue glow intensifies,* **Sarah** *reaches out to the man only she can see*]

Sarah [*holding him*] It's warm in your arms.

[*Pause*]

Sarah Oh I'm not tremblin'!

[*Pause*]

Sarah It's more like melting.

[*She holds him*]

Sarah This is nice, isn't it? Skin to skin.

[*She closes her eyes*]

Sarah Reminds me who I am.

[*She starts to dance with him*]

Sarah I wonder if Mam ever felt this way. I wonder if she ever brimmed over this much.

[*She laughs and opens her eyes*]

Sarah I hardly recognise you.

[*Pause*]

Sarah Maybe I look different. I feel different too.

[**Sarah** *dances slower*]

Sarah Are me eyes glowin'? Am I talkin' slower?

[*Pause*]

Sarah Dancing's good for the soul, that's what Mam always said.

[*Pause*]

Sarah Well it is when y'arms are all full up.

[*Pause*]

Sarah We don't need to talk about that now, just dance wi' me. We've a lot of dancing to do yet.

[*Pause*]

Sarah Mam danced for years after Dad died, said it made her feel he was close.

[*Pause*]

Sarah She looked sad and happy at the same time.

[*Pause*]

Sarah I suppose that's what I'd do.

[*Pause*]

Sarah Dance, like you were still here.

[*Exit* **Girls One**, **Two** *and* **Three**

[**Sarah** *looks around as* **Girls One**, **Two** *and* **Three** *disappear and she dances slower*]

Sarah Where are they going? Why are they fading?

[*Pause*]

Sarah They look pretty. Wouldn't y'say they look pretty?

[*Pause*]

Sarah An' peaceful.

[*The doors open to flood the room with blue light which fades to white as* **Sarah** *dances on*]

Sarah Happiness can be quiet, can't it?

[**Bluebeard** *the man dies*

[**Sarah**'s *arms fall to her side and she looks around at the open doors as the white light fades and the room returns to normal*]

Sarah Sweetheart?

Also by Helena Thompson

The Burning Tower / Ivy

Sarah and Em are best friends who grew up together in West London. Since 2017 they've worked hard researching their estates' past as Living History youth ambassadors. Together they've prepared a presentation on the local heritage of social housing. But Grenfell's shadow threatens the show as the performance space falls into darkness, fuses blow and Sarah starts to panic. Will a mysterious, old latecomer who keeps trying to take over prove a help or a hindrance?

The Burning Tower, a new play by Helena Thompson, is an interactive dramatization of social housing's history. Inspired by interviews with local West London estate residents, it was performed in low tech participatory productions on council estates nationwide before returning to Kensal House Estate.

'*The Burning Tower* is a passionate defence of social housing'
The Guardian

'Moving and passionate'
The Stage

Ivy is an adaptation of Helena Thompson's earlier play *The Burning Times*, commissioned for BBC Radio 4. It was first performed site specifically in collaboration with Southwark Playhouse in 2016. Set in an old building that's about to be demolished, Ivy is a green-fingered old woman who refuses to leave her squat, and whose plants seem to have hallucinogenic powers…

'The tense atmosphere is subtly taken to a new level,
no line in this play is redundant'
Theatre Bubble

'A thrilling script from Thompson; fresh and interesting
work that we all should keep an eye on'
A Younger Theatre

978 0 413 77827 7 / £9.99